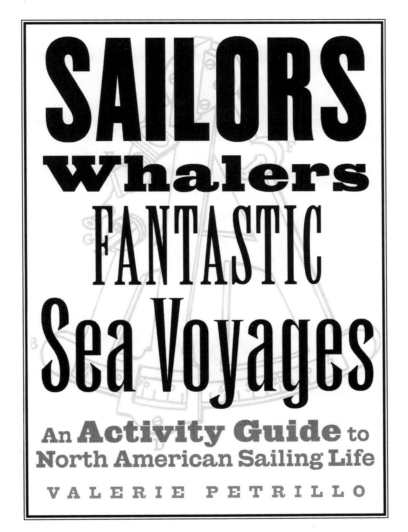

SAILORS Whalers FANTASTIC Sea Voyages

An Activity Guide to North American Sailing Life

VALERIE PETRILLO

CHICAGO REVIEW PRESS

Library of Congress Cataloging-in-Publication Data

Petrillo, Valerie.

    Sailors, whalers, fantastic sea voyages : an activity guide to North American sailing life / Valerie Petrillo.— 1st ed.

      v. cm.

    Includes bibliographical references

    Contents: A sailor's life for me — Shadow box ship — Dandyfunk — Sea chanteys — International signal flags — Make a sailor's tattoo — Be a lookout — Make a sea chest — Collect fresh rainwater — Heave ho! Make a ship's anchor — Make a squeezebox — Dance the sailor's hornpipe — Bean soup — Make a ditty box — King Neptune's visit — There she blows! The whalers — Whaleboat and gear — Plum duff — Iceberg! — Scrimshaw — Walking stick — Keeping the logbook and making a whale stamp — The sea traders — Make a sewing palm — Eight bells and all is well — Lobscouce — Seaweed pictures — Silk — Make a Chinese plate — Chinese tea — Make a bird's nest — Lighthouses — Morse code signal game — Marlinspike — Land ho! Foreign ports — Make a Maori grass skirt — English pedlar doll — Inuit mask — Tangrams — Soapstone carving — Make a Chinese junk — Dragon boats — Baked banana — Flower garland — No'a, a Hawaiian game — Kimo, picking up stones — Feather cape — Sailor's Valentine — Homeward bound: American seaport towns — New England fish chowder — Furl a sail — Make a wharf — Make a barrel — Boston baked beans — Fox and geese — Ropewalk game — Dominoes — Make a figurehead — Jack straws — Wampanoag clam. Casserole Old Maid

    ISBN 1-55652-475-7 1. Seafaring life—Study and teaching—Activity programs—Juvenileliterature. 2. Seafaring life—United States—Study and teaching—Activity programs—Juvenile literature. [1. Seafaring life.] I. Title.

G540.P48 2003   910.4'5—dc21

2002153646

Cover design: Joan Sommers Design
Cover photos: Oil painting on canvas by Montague Dawson, privately owned; black and white photograph, left, Men at rail of bark *Alice*, ca. 1900, © Mystic Seaport, Mystic, CT; and color image, right, Circa Art Image no. 725537, Getty Images.
Interior design: Rattray Design
Interior illustration: Laura D'Argo and Valerie Petrillo

First edition
Published by Chicago Review Press, Incorporated
814 North Franklin Street
Chicago, Illinois 60610
ISBN 1-55652-475-7
Printed in the United States of America
5 4 3 2 1

With love to my home crew: to Hank, my patient, encouraging husband, who now knows more about whaling than the Red Sox (well, almost). To my kids who lived with harpoons in the kitchen, lobscouse for supper, icebergs in the freezer, and a shortage of clean towels. Love and thanks to Mike, who offered artistic help and guidance; Nick, who cheerfully kid-tested the activities; and Noelle, the other writer in the family, who always liked Mom's stories best. And, finally, to my sister Norma, who listens and makes me laugh.

Contents

Acknowledgments

Thanks to editor Cynthia Sherry for giving me this wonderful opportunity. I'm especially grateful to my project editor, Lisa Rosenthal, who shared my enthusiasm for the subject and helped me develop and elevate the manuscript into a strong and engaging book. Many thanks to Chicago Review Press publisher Linda Matthews, who carefully reviewed the pages and nurtured the progress of the book; Gerilee Hundt, managing editor, who put together a great team to bring the book to life; Meg Cox, a meticulous copyeditor; and Allison Felus, editorial assistant, who worked on the book in all stages of the production process.

I would like to express my appreciation for the lovely artwork and design of the book. Thank you to Laura A. D'Argo for her delightful illustrations, Scott Rattray of Rattray Design who created the layout of the book, Joan Sommers of Joan Sommers Design for designing the magnificent cover, and Michael Petrillo for his artistic help in the step-by-step instructions.

Many thanks to Heather Shanks and Carolle Morini at the Peabody Essex Museum and Dana Costanza from the Martha's Vineyard Historical Society. Thanks also to Peter Kerner and his "nautical sense" for checking parts of the manuscript for authenticity.

I'd also like to offer my thanks and appreciation to all the maritime museums and volunteers in our country who work hard to allow us to step back to the days of clipper ships and harpoons.

Special thanks to our wonderful big extended family, who have been incredibly supportive, as well as encouraging in my writing all these years, and finally to my late parents, Hermione and Charles Mears—to Dad who could make anything with a piece of wood and a few nails, and to Mom, whose stories of the past made history come alive.

Time Line

4,000 years ago
Native Americans catch whales that wash ashore and use canoes to capture whales along the shallow coastline.

1620
Mayflower lands at Plymouth Rock. Settlers hunt whales right from shore.

1750
Tryworks first used onboard a whaleship.

1784
The *Empress of China* enters the anchorage of Whampoa to trade with the Chinese.

1793
Pacific whaling begins when the *Rebecca* rounds Cape Horn to deliver a full cargo of sperm whale oil home to New Bedford.

1640
First organized whale fishery, Long Island, New York.

1712
Sperm whaling begins off the coast of Massachusetts.

1776
America declares independence from England. British blockade colonial ports during the Revolutionary War and bring whaling to a halt.

1859
Petroleum oil discovered in Pennsylvania. Kerosene begins to replace whale oil for lighting fuel.

1869
First transcontinental railroad is complete.

1924
On August 25 the last whaler, the *Wanderer*, sails out from New Bedford, Massachusetts.

1808
Congress outlaws American participation in the African slave trade.

1818
The first American packet ship, *James Monroe* of the Black Ball line, sails from New York to Liverpool.

1845
The *Rainbow*, the first American clipper ship, is launched.

1856
Harpoon gun is invented.

1871
Thirty-three whalers lost, trapped in Arctic ice.

1802
First steamboat launched in England.

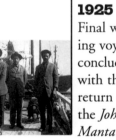

1812
War of 1812. British impress American ships and force crews into naval service. Americans respond by recapturing ships and crippling the British fleet.

1841
Fresnel lighthouse lens is used.

1848
Gold discovered in California.

Lewis Temple invents toggle iron harpoon.

Whalers enter Bering Sea, Arctic.

1854
Clipper ship *Lightning*, built by Donald McKay, sets a world record by traveling 436 nautical miles in one day.

1861
Civil War devastates whaling and merchant fleet. Confederates burn and sink 40 ships.

1925
Final whaling voyage concludes with the return of the *John R. Manta*.

Introduction

Imagine yourself at the bow of a sailing ship, the ocean spray on your face and the endless blue horizon ahead. You are a sailor beginning a three-year deepwater journey across the world. What will you take with you? Who will you leave behind? Do you think you'll return alive?

The seafaring life was a challenging one in the 19th century—whaling ships searched the seven seas for whales that yielded precious oil and bone. Merchant ships, with their tall sails and sleek shapes, rushed to trade cargo from foreign ports to America's shores.

Maritime history covers many subjects: naval history, fishing, inland waterways, commerce, exploration, adventure, and whaling. *Sailors, Whalers, Fantastic Sea Voyages: An Activity Guide to North American Sailing Life* takes you on a journey to learn about North America's deepwater sailors: whalemen and merchant seamen who made their living from the sea, and whose jobs took them away for months and years at a time.

Our story begins with the daily life of the sailor. We sail with him as we learn about the clothes he wore, the food he ate, and the superstitions he held—about everything from sailing on Friday to losing a bucket overboard. Then we'll make some sailor's

Clipper ship *Three Brothers*, 2,972 tons (2,696 metric tons). *Library of Congress*

crafts, from shadow box ships to sea chests. We'll hear stories about children who grew up on sailing ships and take a peek in the *galley*, the ship's kitchen. We'll even try our hand at making *dandyfunk*, a sailor's snack.

In Chapter 2 we move on to the life of the whalemen and experience the heart-pounding excitement of the whale hunt. We'll watch as a sailor goes from *greenhand*, a new recruit, to *old salt*, an experienced sailor. You'll see why the whale was so valuable in early America and how its oil lit the lamps of the world. Along the way you'll see how whaling pro-

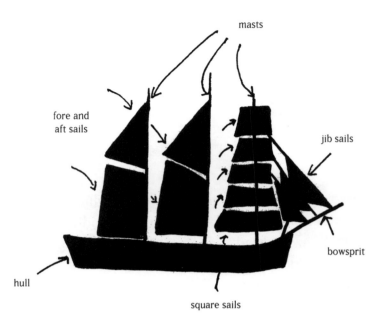

Parts of a Sailing Ship

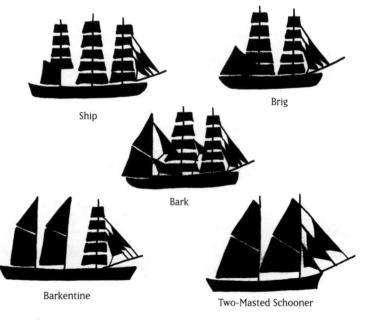

Types of Sailing Ships

gressed from coastal whaling in canoes to deepwater whaling in large wooden sailing ships. Then we'll join the crew to mold a set of whale stamps, which the whalemen used to record their sightings, and stroll into port with a whalebone walking stick.

The sea traders follow in Chapter 3—you'll explore the lives and work of America's merchant sailors. We'll accompany them as they sail across the oceans in magnificent clipper ships in search of all that the world has to offer. Our trip takes us from China for silk, tea, and porcelain to seeking bird's nests in the cliffs of Borneo. We'll come face to face with real pirates; eat *lobscouse*, an authentic sailor's dinner; and make a sewing palm for mending sails.

In Chapter 4, foreign ports beckon. This chapter is about the sailor on *liberty*—free time during which the sailors were allowed to leave the ship. Join the sailors as they see the sights, taste the foods, play the games, and experience the cultures of different seaports around the world. Sailors were also tourists, buying or trading for native crafts that they brought home. Make an English pedlar (that's how they spelled it!) doll, or a Maori grass skirt from the Bay of Islands; join in the Hawaiian game of kimo, or test your visual skills with Chinese tangrams.

Chapter 5 ends this book and focuses on the sailor coming home. It was quite an event when deepwater sailors returned from sea, for they had often been gone for two or three years! This chapter lets us in on the life of the sailor at home. You'll learn some of the many old-fashioned American games he played, such as fox and geese, dominoes, ropewalk, and jack straws. You'll also learn about the crafts of the seaport: sail making, barrel making, and figurehead carving.

Throughout the book you'll find interesting facts about seafaring life kept safe inside a treasure chest. What really happened to Captain Cook and why sailors didn't believe in learning to swim are some of the treasure in this chest.

You'll also find an extensive resource section so you can learn more about seafaring life. There is a glossary of nautical words, a list of maritime museums and historic lighthouses you can visit, a listing of seafaring Web sites, and even a list of seaworthy movies.

Now off we go to our high sea adventures!

1

A Sailor's Life for Me!

W hat was it like to be a sailor? This chapter will give you a chance to climb onboard a sailing ship and experience life through the eyes of a greenhand. The daily life of a deepwater sailor was passed down from generations of men who made their living from the sea. Join us on our voyage as we learn to talk like sailors, eat sailor's grub, sing sea chanteys, and dance the sailor's hornpipe. We'll hear the story of a mutiny, make a ship's anchor, and take a turn as a lookout. When we cross the equator, King Neptune will visit us. Then we can relax in our bunks, maybe get a sailor's tattoo or make a squeezebox to play.

Who were the sailors? The majority were young. Some shipped out in their teens, but most were in their early twenties when they headed out to sea. Shipping accounts reveal that half of most crews were first-time sailors as opposed to the old salts we often think of from folklore. For many of these men, shipping out to sea

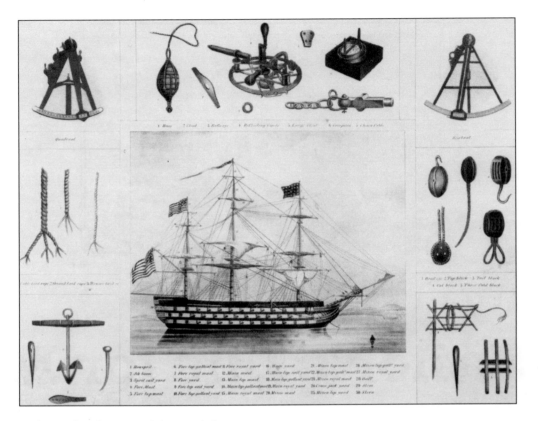

A ship and its furniture. *Library of Congress*

was the first time they had been away from home. They struggled with terrible homesickness as they dealt with the tremendous physical and emotional demands of becoming a sailor.

The young seamen were seeking adventure and employment, and trying to prove themselves as men. As for the old salts, they simply saw no other way to make a living, so as soon as one voyage ended they shipped out on another. These men's wives lived as widows and their children grew up without fathers. There were so many female-run businesses in the seaport of Nantucket, Massachusetts, that one street was nicknamed *Petticoat Row*. And when the children of these old salts followed their fathers to the call of the sea, it was their mothers and grandmothers they pined for.

Build a Shadow Box Ship

The ship was the sailor's entire world for months and years at a time. It was his home, his transportation, his shelter from the mighty ocean, his workplace, and his place to socialize. Of all sailors' hobbies, the building of model ships was the most popular. They carved model ships out of wood, whalebone, or ivory, and sewed the sails with scraps of canvas tied with rope and string. The sailor used whatever materials were available to him.

The shadow box was a popular 19th-century art form, and ship models were often displayed this way. Make a model of the ship known as a bark. This type of ship was commonly used for whaling.

What You Need

A grown-up to assist
Blue construction paper
Scissors
Sturdy shallow box,
    13 inches (33.02 centimeters) high by 15 inches (38.1 centimeters) wide or larger
Glue stick
Pencil
1 white 12-inch (30.48 centimeters) by 18-inch (45.72 centimeters) by 2-millimeters-thick craft foam sheet (available in craft stores)
Hole punch

4 wooden dowels, ¼ inch (6.35 millimeters) thick by 12 inches (30.48 centimeters) long (available in craft stores)
Knife (for adult use)
Sturdy string (such as kite string)
Glue
1 black 12-inch (30.48 centimeters) by 18-inch (45.72 centimeters) by 2-millimeters-thick craft foam sheet
Pen
2 brass fasteners

What You Do

1. Cut the construction paper to fit the inside bottom of the box.
2. Glue the paper down with the glue stick.
3. Pencil the shapes from the templates below onto the white foam and cut out. You will need two each of the square sails in the first column, one each of the sails in the middle column, and five of the long triangular sails in the last column.
4. Punch holes where shown.
5. Weave the dowels through the top and bottom of each sail to match the picture.
6. Ask an adult to cut the fourth dowel in half. Use one of the pieces as a *bowsprit* (the sideways spar).
7. Tie the triangular sails to the dowels with the string.
8. Glue the dowels to the construction paper. Do not glue down the sails or string.
9. Pinch the top and bottom of the sails together so that they billow out away from the box. Let dry.
10. Cut a 15-inch (38.1-centimeter) by 2½-inch (6.35-centimeter) piece of black foam for the bottom of the ship. Lay the foam across the bottom of the box and push each side in about 1 inch (2.54 centimeters) so that it pops out.
11. With the point of a pen, push a hole through the top inside left corner of the foam and the box underneath. Do the same to the other side.
12. Attach to the box with the fasteners. Display upright.

4

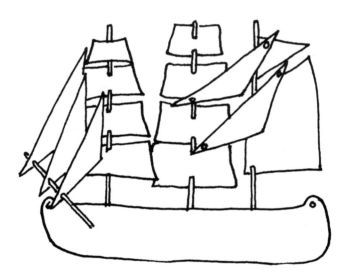

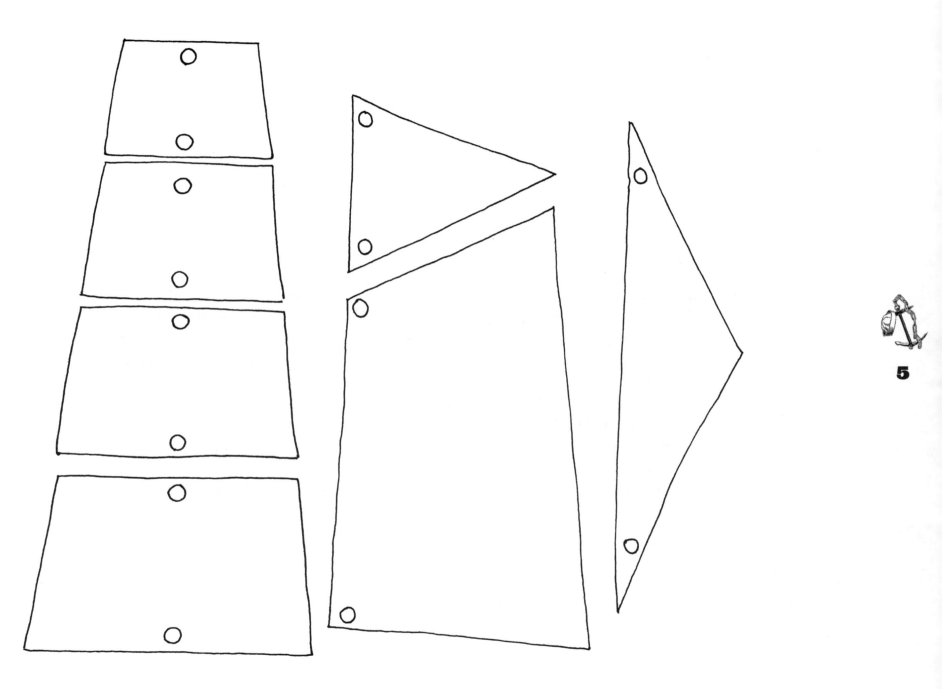

5

Salty Language

Imagine how a greenhand felt when the first mate pointed to a skyful of sails and rigging and issued this command: "Boy, git aout on th' jib-boom an' take th'gaskets off'n th'jib an' jib-tops'l!" Would you know what to do? What the mate said was, "Boy, get out on that *jib-boom* (a long pole that extends under a sail) and take the *gaskets* (cords) off the *jib* (the foremost sail of the ship) and *jib topsail* (a sail higher up on the *stay* (rope)."

Learning the specialized lingo of a sailing ship was almost like learning a foreign language. Every chore, rope, mast, and sail had its own particular name. Not understanding this language could have dire—even life-threatening—consequences.

Today nautical speech has so permeated American culture that it has become a common part of our language. The seafaring roots of expressions such as "hit the deck," "don't rock the boat," "stay on an even keel," "any port in a storm," "not on my watch," and "taking the wind out of one's sails" are easy to see. Here are some other salty sayings that you can practice on your own or share with your friends.

Expression	Old Meaning	New Meaning
Let the cat out of the bag	The *cat-o'-nine-tails* was a knotted leather rope used to flog men aboard ship. Letting the cat out of the bag meant that the rope was soon to be used on a sailor who had misbehaved.	To reveal a secret
Scuttlebutt	A cask with a hole cut for drinking. Near the scuttlebutt was a popular place aboard ship to gather and socialize.	Gossip or rumor
Try a different tack	To try setting the sails differently relative to the direction of the wind.	To look at something in a new way, to try a different approach
Fly-by-night	A large sail that could only be used when sailing downwind. It was used at night in place of several smaller sails, requiring less work and attention from the crew.	Hastily or poorly thrown together, unprofessional
Taken aback	When the wind shifts suddenly and passes from the back of the sails to the front, taking the ship backward.	Surprised
Footloose	When the bottom of the sail (the foot) is not attached to the boom and it dances in the wind.	Free and unattached

---

These sayings are unique to the sailors.

Expression	Meaning
Always ready to rig his yarn tackle	Loves to tell stories
Through the hawsehole	The way an officer who has worked his way up from the bottom got his job
Square the yards with	To get even with someone
In everybody's mess and nobody's watch	Lazy, a fair-weather friend
The cut of one's jib	A person's appearance

Nautical Terms

Anchor cable A heavy rope or chain used to raise or lower the anchor

Bow The front of the ship

Cask Barrel for holding liquids

Downwind With the wind

Flog To whip

Hawsehole An opening in the bow of the ship through which the anchor cable passes

Keel The backbone of the ship, the timber the ship is built upon

Mast A long pole or spar that rises vertically from the deck and carries sails, yards, and rigging

Mess A group of men who eat or lodge together

Nautical Related to the sea

Pitch The alternate dipping of the bow and stern, the movement of the ship

Port A harbor; also, the left side of the ship as you face forward

Rig To fit or equip. Also the arrangement of masts, sails, and rigging that determine the vessel type.

Rigging All the lines, chains, and tackle above deck that are used to control the sails

Starboard The right side of a ship as you face forward

Stern The rear of the ship

Watch A part of the crew that shares duties together. It also means the four-hour block of time in which part of the crew is working and the rest of the crew is off.

Yard A long spar or pole tied to a mast, which supports the spread of a sail

Sailor Suits: What the Seamen Wore

erchant seamen did not have uniforms, but their clothing was similar to navy garb. Pants were bell-bottomed, a style that was particularly well suited to seafaring life because they could be rolled up easily when the deck was wet. Shirts were either blousy red- or blue-checked tunics or tight-fitting wool shirts called *guernseys*. For tarring the rigging and other messy jobs, they wore duck shirts made of old canvas sail. Sailors and their clothes were so often covered with tar that they referred to each other as *Jack Tar*.

Whalers wore about anything they could find. Their clothes were soon beaten and weathered by months of saltwater and whale oil. Holes were mended and patched and mended again. By the voyage's end everything was in tatters and usually had to be thrown away. In cold weather sailors wore red flannel underwear. Waterproof *oilskin* suits and hats protected them on deck during storms. The sailors made these suits themselves out of canvas that had been soaked in oil or tar. If they were lucky they had leather sea boots that they slathered with grease and tar to protect them from the saltwater.

The most popular sailor's hat was the black tarred tarpaulin hat, cocked to the back and trailing a foot or two of black ribbon. It was waterproof and tough enough to stand up to the wind and salt, and it didn't show the dirt. In warmer climates sailors wore the straw-braided sennit hat. They wore stocking caps in the winter. During the later days of sailing, caps with visors came into fashion. Most seamen wore square-knotted black kerchiefs around their neck as well.

On land sailors wore their best clothes: baggy white trousers, cotton broad-collared shirts, and navy jackets or pea coats. This name derives from the short double-breasted coat called the *pijjekker*, which was worn by Dutch sailors. On land sailors wore shoes! Most sailors worked barefoot when they were on the ship because shoes got too wet and slippery.

Sailor's Grub

"Rancid meat, putrid water, and wormy bread." That's what a menu on a sailing ship would read if it was accurate. For hardworking men so far from home, shipboard meals offered little comfort. Salted beef, pork, and fish; beans; rice; potatoes; and hardtack made up the seaboard staples. *Hardtack*, or sea biscuit, is very dry and hard, but it lasts for months, even years, without spoiling. The meat was tough and so salty that when it was put in a cask of seawater to soften it actually became *less* salty!

At the outset of the voyage there was plenty of clean water, livestock for fresh meat, and vegetables such as potatoes, carrots, and cabbage. But as the journey wore on, the water began to stink and became foul tasting, the livestock were consumed, and the vegetable supply dwindled or ran out completely. The food that remained became infested with weevils and cockroaches. Once in a while food from the sea was harvested, such as flying fish, porpoise, and sea turtle, but it often went only to the officers' table. The best relief from the shipboard diet was a trip into a port, such as a Pacific island where luscious fruits and vegetables grew in abundance.

The captain, his family, and the ship's officers in the *cabin* (their living quarters) ate quite differently from the poor sailors. They sat at a table and ate their meals with silverware and china. Cabin food was of a better quality and quantity. It consisted of more fresh meats, fruits, and vegetables. It also included little luxuries such as cheese, butter, soft bread, pickles, sugar, and desserts. This difference in the dining experience often led to hard feelings between the crew and the officers. Many a mutiny at sea began with a bad meal.

Sailors gave their own names to the food that they ate: salt beef was called salt horse and salt pork was salt junk. Molasses was called long-tailed sugar because it was used as a cheap substitute for sugar and when it was cold, it turned into a thick black paste. The biscuits were called hardtack, soft bread was soft tack, and all food was *grub*.

The sailor's favorite foods were *lobscouse*, a stew of pounded hardtack, meat, and potatoes; sea pie, a flour dumpling with meat and ground porpoise bones; and *duff* or *plum duff*, a dessert served once or twice a week. Duff was a flour pudding made with raisins or sea-dried apples, boiled in a cloth bag, and served with molasses sauce. Once in a while, if the cook allowed them into the galley, sailors made a special treat called *dandyfunk*, made of pounded hardtack and molasses.

At mealtime usually the youngest sailor was sent to the galley to bring the food back to the *fo'c'sle* (*forecastle*, pronounced "fokesull"). This was the common sailors' living quarters, located beneath deck in the front of the ship.

The food was served in a big wooden tub with iron hoops, called a *kid* (maybe named for the young person who carried it). The kid was placed on the floor and the men gathered around, digging into it with pocketknives and spoons to fill their tin plates.

Mutiny out of New Bedford

On July 21, 1857, a ship known as the *Junior* sailed out of New Bedford bound for the bowhead whaling grounds of the Sea of Okhotsk, near Japan. The voyage began badly because of the horrible food the sailors were served. There were three casks of moldy bread and a large amount of rotting meat filled with maggots left over from a previous voyage. Finally, when it became so bad that the men fell ill, 24-year-old Cyrus Plummer and the other men of his watch went straight to Captain Archibald Mellen to complain.

Plummer was a *boatsteerer* and harpooner, who harpooned the whale, then sat in the back of the whaleboat and steered. He was not afraid of whale or man. The mistake he made was to go over the head of his superior officer, Chief Mate William Nelson, which angered Nelson.

The chief mate got an opportunity to retaliate one day when Plummer was standing watch at the wheel. Plummer had become fascinated watching the flight of an albatross, an enormous seabird. His reverie caused him to sail slightly off course, and Nelson was there to witness it. The mate approached and smashed Plummer in the jaw. Not one to back down from a fight, Plummer retaliated and they fought on deck. When Plummer fell and hit his head, Nelson took advantage of the situation and kicked him mercilessly. Finally the captain broke it up.

Plummer was punished for the crime of *insubordination*, speaking back to or striking an officer. He was hung by his thumbs in the rigging and given 20 lashes with a cat-o'-nine-tails by Chief Mate Nelson.

Plummer recovered, but he became obsessed with taking over the ship. He conspired with a group of sailors and they came up with a plan. On Christmas night, 1857, Plummer and nine of his crew members declared mutiny. They killed all the officers aboard except the first mate. They allowed the first mate to navigate the ship to Australia. The mutineers left in two whaleboats loaded with supplies. After they reached the coast, they bickered and split up. Six were captured within days, but Plummer and the three others in his group managed to make it to Sydney. After a night of drunken escapades, Plummer's fellow mutineers were arrested in a tavern and eventually sentenced to six years in prison in the United States. Plummer escaped through an open window, but was arrested a few days later for stealing gold with a new gang he had fallen in with. While in jail he heard that two of the mutineers had been hanged at Port Albert, Australia.

Cyrus Plummer was brought back to the United States and sentenced to hang on June 24, 1859. Just hours before he was to be executed, the lucky mutineer's sentence was commuted to life imprisonment by President James Buchanan. Fifteen years later, an aged and ailing Plummer was granted a pardon by President Ulysses S. Grant. On July 24, 1874, he walked out of prison to freedom.

Make Dandyfunk

aving a snack when he wanted to was a comfort denied to the common sailor. Meals were served at precise times and carefully rationed. One of the few foods that was off ration (they could have as much as they wanted) was hardtack,* the dry sea biscuit. If a sailor saved a spoon or two of his molasses from dinner and bargained with the cook for some slush (leftover drippings from cooked meat), he could mix it with the hardtack to make a sweet treat for himself.

Note: Hardtack is available in Newfoundland, Nova Scotia, and other parts of Canada. In the United States you can purchase it from Bent's Cookie Factory in Massachusetts (www.bentscookiefactory.com). Nabisco makes the same cracker under the name Crown Pilot Crackers (sold in the Northeast). The Mechanical Baking Company in Illinois also sells hardtack (www.mechanical-bakery.com).

What You Need

Paper towel
Approximately 1 tablespoon (15 millileters) shortening, such as Crisco or butter
Small baking dish
1 cup (56 grams) of crushed crackers, such as saltines

1-gallon (3.78-liter) resealable plastic bag
Drinking glass
⅛ cup (60 milliliters) light molasses
2 tablespoons (30 grams) butter
Fork

What You Do

1. Preheat the oven to 350°F. (176.67°C).
2. Dip the paper towel into the shortening can and scoop out a tablespoon-size amount. Use this to grease the baking dish.
3. Place the crackers in the bag, seal it, and roll over it with the glass until the crackers are coarsely crushed.
4. Pour the crackers into the baking dish and mix in the molasses and butter with a fork.
5. Bake for 15 minutes.

Yield: 4 servings

Hen Frigates: Women and Children at Sea

Dear Ezra,
Where did you put the ax?
Love,
Martha

The answer to this note arrived in Nantucket 14 months later:

Dear Martha,
What do you want the ax for?
Love,
Ezra

Ezra received his answer on the Pacific Ocean one year later:

Dear Ezra,
Never mind about the ax. What did you do with the hammer?
Love,
Martha

With their husbands at sea for years at a time, most Yankee wives had to adapt to a self-sufficient life. They attended to all household duties, raised the children by themselves, and took care of their husbands' businesses as well. A typical whaleman was at home for only 20 months out of 10 years—that's an average of 2 months per year!

In the 1800s many captains' wives set out to sea with their husbands and took their children along. They were the only wives allowed to join the ship. This was good news for the crew because on *hen frigates*, as the sailors called these ships, sailors generally received less harsh discipline than when there was no woman aboard. The crew also behaved better. Hen frigates seemed to bring out the best in the captain as well as his men.

Even though the conditions at times could be quite squalid, especially aboard a whaling ship—the stench of boiling blubber, the decks awash with blood and oil, the brutal killing of whales, isolation from friends and relatives—these families were willing to make sacrifices to be together. Seagoing families tried hard to create a decent home life within these unusual conditions. Women decorated their cabins with plants, carpets, figurines, and photographs.

Many mothers gave birth while at sea. Although the rolling of the ship might lull a baby to sleep, it must have been a nightmare for a mother chasing a toddler!

The day started with breakfast in the cabin with mother, father, children, and the officers at seven bells (7:30). They ate at a table that had a lip around the edge and was divided into three sections by long boards called fiddles. The fiddles were a couple of inches tall and ran lengthwise down the middle. This prevented the plates from sliding off the table when the ship pitched up and down.

Because of the crew's division of labor aboard ship, deepwater women enjoyed relative freedom from domestic duties. The cook prepared all the meals, which the *steward* served and cleaned up after. The steward also did the polishing, sweeping, and washing in the cabin. This left the captain's wife with a lot more free time than she would have had at home. Her days onboard were typically spent taking care of children, doing the family's laundry, sewing, reading, writing letters, and keeping a journal. Many

wives at sea also tended to the sick, even stitching up sailors after injuries.

Mothers aboard ship were also responsible for their children's education in reading, writing, and arithmetic. Keeping up with these lessons was a challenge. Book learning often collided with the stunning real-life lessons aboard ship: riding out storms, trading in foreign lands, whale hunting and processing, trips into port, and the spectacle of operating the square rigger.

Children were quick to pick up navigational skills as well, and most were taught how to *shoot the sun*. This meant measuring the altitude of the sun with an instrument know as a *sextant*. This number was then looked up on a navigational table to locate the ship's geographical position. At daybreak children eagerly scanned the horizon with their father's spyglass to see what vessels had passed in the night.

During storms, the children were sent below to the captain's quarters while the crew worked furiously above. They could hear the men yelling above the roar of the sea, and the pounding of boots across the decks. It must have been exciting but scary to watch the white foamy waves through the tiny windows below, and to keep themselves from sliding as the ship pitched.

They spent their free time exploring the ship, being careful not to wake sleeping men whose watch was over. Although they were prohibited from interfering or socializing with the crew, the children were drawn to the men's work. They watched from a distance as sailors worked the thousands of yards of rope, and they learned how to tie a bowline, the most useful knot used aboard ship; how to tie ropes together by using a sheet bend knot; and how to splice, or weave, two ropes into one.

After rough weather, the decks were white with great clouds of canvas to be repaired. When no one was watching, it made a great place to hide or make a tent.

Little children found it fun to pitch things overboard or to climb up the forbidden rigging. These antics more often than not brought a smile to the sailors' faces. Many a *scrimshaw* (design carved into whalebone) gift made its way from the sailors' fo'c'sle to the children. In the evenings, if there wasn't a whale to be chased or *cut in* (its blubber removed), the family spent the time playing cards, dominoes, backgammon, and cribbage.

Children were not spared the harshness of seafaring life. They witnessed men falling overboard, people (including themselves) suffering serious injuries, shipboard floggings, shipwrecks, and mutinies. They made pets of the pigs, hens, and chickens aboard ship—and were understandably upset when a pet was slaughtered and served for dinner!

Although isolation was a major problem, deepwater children were far worldlier than their contemporaries at home. They were among the first Americans to visit exotic Pacific islands, South America, Australia, Asia, and the Arctic. At the height of whaling, Honolulu became a home away from home for whaling families. They settled in for weeks or months at a time, visiting, gathering fresh provisions, and making repairs on the ship. Sometimes they sold their oil to merchant ships returning home, and the wives and children stayed while the ship went on to hunt bowhead whales in the Arctic. These whales were plentiful in the Arctic during the second half of the 19th century, and yielded valuable oil and *baleen* (whale cartilage). Many families remained on the ships and traveled to the Arctic despite the ice and the bitter storms of the northern seas.

Returning home could be a difficult adjustment for these children. They frequently became sick with illnesses their travels had protected them from catching. Captains' children who had learned to walk aboard a rolling ship sometimes had trouble adjusting to walking on land! Older children were surprised to realize that their clothes had gone out of style.

Despite the hardships and isolation, many of the children who had spent time at sea went on to become harpooners, craftsmen, officers, and captains of their own ships. We learn about their experiences through their memoirs. Many refer to those years as the best of their lives.

A Child's Journal

To learn about what it was like to be a child aboard a whaler, read *A Whaling Captain's Daughter: The Diary of Laura Jernegan 1868–1871.*

The journal describes **Laura Jernegan's** family's voyage aboard the whaler *Roman.* Their trip took them from **New Bedford, Massachusetts,** around the tip of **South America** to **Honolulu.** Laura was six and her little brother Prescott was two when their journey began. Here is a typical entry from her journal:

Tuesday 21st 1871—

It is quite pleasant today, the men are cutting in the whales, they smel dredfully, we got a whale that made 75 barrels [.] the whales head made 20 barrels of oil. the whales head is as big as four whole rooms, and his body as long as one ship. the men have got 5 whales cut in, they have throne [thrown] some of the whale overboard. it is fun to see them cut the whales in. Mama has just come doon [down] stairs, and Prescott and I just went up on deck and the men were just geting the last peice [piece]. when they get done they all hury, hury and five and forty More. Papa said that he would put some whales down in my journal, but I don't think so. Prescott is up on deck, I am going up on deck. the men have just begun to boil out the blubber.

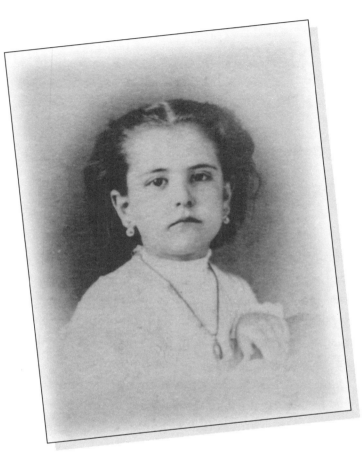

Laura Jernegan, between six and eight years old here.
Martha's Vineyard Historical Society

17

Sea Chanteys

The work of a sailor was hard and monotonous. To break up the drudgery, sailors often sang. The *sea chantey* is a combination chant and song that kept the men working in harmony and seemed to lighten the load. The old salts used to say, "a good chantey is another hand on the rope." The chantey was led by a *chanteyman*. Sailors chose their own chanteyman, usually a good-natured sailor with a robust voice and a sense of humor.

As with everything else aboard ship, each chantey had a specific purpose. Short-haul chanteys were for hauling jobs that required a few strong pulls. Halyard chanteys were used for jobs that required a longer period of labor. They were named after the *halyard*, the line used for raising and lowering sails. Raising a 1,000- or 2,000-pound (454- or 907-kilogram) sail required team effort, and this chantey was designed for the sailors to rest during the verse and haul during the chorus. Capstan chanteys were used for long rhythmic tasks such as pulling up an anchor with a mechanical device known as a *capstan*. The sailors walked in a circle pushing the bars, stamping and singing as they pulled up the anchor. The lifting of the anchor could take several hours.

Here are some popular chanteys. You may have heard different versions of these, which is natural for a folk song. A folk song is like a family recipe—everybody puts in a little of this and a little of that to make it his or her own. Make up your own tune to these lyrics.

The chanteyman called out the verses and the rest of the sailors answered with the chorus:

Haul on the Bowlin'

(short-haul chantey)

Haul on the bowlin'
Our bully ship's a 'rollin'!
Haul on the bowlin'
The bowlin', haul!

Haul on the bowlin'
Our captain he's a 'growlin'
Haul on the bowlin'
The bowlin', haul!

Haul on the bowlin'
O Kitty, you're my darlin'
Haul on the bowlin'
The bowlin', haul!

"Blow the Man Down" is a chantey about the sailors who worked on the Black Ball line, the first line of *packet ships* to take mail and passengers on a regular schedule from Boston, New York, and Philadelphia to Liverpool, England, and back. The ships were fast and efficient. They were known for their captains' cruel and demanding treatment of the sailors.

Blow the Man Down

(halyard chantey, 1849)

Come all ya young fellers that follow the sea
With a ho, ho, blow the man down
Now just pay attention and listen to me
Give me some time to blow the man down

Aboard the Black Baller I first served my time
With a ho, ho, blow the man down
But on the Black Baller I wasted my time
Give me some time to blow the man down

There's tinkers and tailors and sailors and all
With a ho, ho, blow the man down
That sailed for good seamen aboard the Black Ball
Give me some time to blow the man down

'Tis larboard and starboard, on deck you will crawl
With a ho, ho, blow the man down
When kicking Jack Williams commands the Black Ball
Give me some time to blow the man down

Now when the Black Baller's preparin' for sea
With a ho, ho, blow the man down
You'd bust your sides laughin' at sights that you see
Give me some time to blow the man down

(continued)

19

But when the Black Baller is clear of the land
With a ho, ho, blow the man down
Old kicking Jack Williams gives ev'ry command
Give me some time to blow the man down

Aboard the Black Baller I first served my time
With a ho ho blow the man down
But on the Black Baller I wasted my time
Give me some time to blow the man down

"Shenandoah" is an American sea chantey. It tells the story of a trader falling in love with the Indian chief Shenandoah's daughter.

Shenandoah
(capstan chantey, 1837)

Oh, Shenandoah, I long to hear you
Away you rolling river
Oh Shenandoah, I long to hear you
Away, I'm bound away

Cross the wide Missouri
Oh, Shenandoah, I love your daughter
Away you rolling river
I'll take her 'cross that rolling water
Away, I'm bound away
'Cross the wide Missouri

This white man loves your Indian maiden
Away you rolling river
In my canoe with notions laden
Away, I'm bound away
'Cross the wide Missouri

Farewell, goodbye, I shall not grieve you
Away you rolling river
Oh, Shenandoah, I'll not deceive you
Away, we're bound away
'Cross the wide Missouri

International Signal Flags

Before the age of electronic radio transmissions, ships used flags to communicate with other ships or with the shore. Flags sent different messages depending on their design, color, or placement on the rigging. Signal flags could mean the difference between life and death if a ship was sinking, or if a vessel needed to be warned of danger ahead (such as an iceberg). A universal language of the sea was created so that nations could communicate with each other.

The International Code of Signals was developed in 1855. With several revisions, it is used to this day by most seafaring nations. It allows any ship that carries the published book of codes to decipher a message, even if the crew members don't speak the language of the sender.

Man Overboard!

A sailor falling from the decks or rigging of a slippery, pitching ship and into the sea below was fairly common. Surprisingly many sailors didn't know how to swim. They felt that the agony of being shipwrecked would be worse than drowning. When the shout of "Man overboard!" came, a line was immediately hoisted over the side of the ship. With luck the sailor was near enough to climb back aboard.

Each flag has two meanings—an English letter as well as a message. For instance, the letter *O* also means "man overboard." If the only way to send a message were the letter-by-letter method, it would take a lot of flags to send a long message.

Why do we need the International Signal Code when we have high-tech radio and satellite communications?

International signal code flags are still used in heavily trafficked international shipping lanes and by the U.S. Navy and Coast Guard. These flags are important for silent communication when vessels do not want their messages to be intercepted. Ships also use them in emergency situations when radio communication breaks down. Today sailing ships enjoy displaying these flags in an arch from stern to bow for special occasions such as the Fourth of July.

International Signal Flags
Alphabet and Code Pennants

A
Diver Down
Keep Clear

B
Dangerous
Cargo

C
Yes

D
Keep Clear

E
Altering Course
to Starboard

F
Disabled

G
Require a
Pilot

H
Pilot on
Board

I
Altering Course
to Port

J
On Fire
Keep Clear

K
Desire to
Communicate

L
Stop
Immediately

M
I Am
Stopped

N
No

O
Man
Overboard

P
About to
Sail

Q
Request to
Use Port

R
No
Meaning

S
Engines Going
Astern

T
Do Not Pass
Ahead of Me

U
Standing into
Danger

V
Require
Assistance

W
Require Medical
Assistance

X
Stop Your
Intention

Y
I Am Dragging
Anchor

Z
Require a
Tug

= red   = blue

= yellow   = white

= black

Spelling Out Messages with International Signal Flags

Here is an example of how a message would be displayed on a ship. Each word would be hoisted vertically on a separate flagpole so it could be read from top to bottom. The letter flags for Y and Z on the first flagpole mean that the message is spelled out.

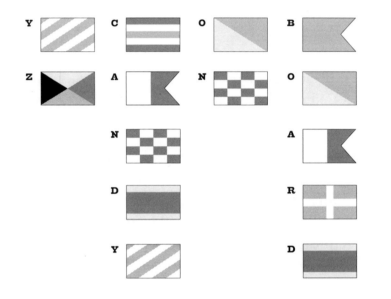

The message says "CANDY ONBOARD."

Sending Coded Messages with International Signal Flags

A — If this flag were hoisted by itself it would mean "Diver Down. Keep Clear." and not the letter A. There is no need for YZ because the message is in code and not spelled out.

A

C — If you saw these two flags together it would not mean AC. It would also not mean "Diver Down. Keep Clear." or "Yes." It would have an entirely different message that you could decode only with a special book of international signals written in your language. This message means "I am abandoning my vessel."

Try decoding this spelled out message. The answer is on page 25.

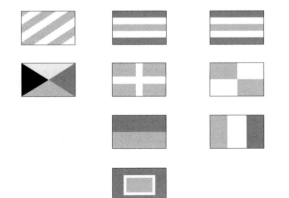

23

Superstitions

Sailors at sea for months and years experienced the extremes of Mother Nature. One day they could be basking in tropical sunsets and balmy breezes and the next day they could be fighting for their lives in gale-force winds and 50-foot waves. Over the years sailors developed superstitious behaviors and rituals that helped them cope with the unpredictability of their world. Here are some.

Fridays: It was considered bad luck to commence a voyage on a Friday because it is said to be the day Christ was crucified.

Whistling: Sailors whistled to summon a wind in calm seas, but otherwise it was prohibited for fear of attracting a gale.

Rats: If rats left a ship when it was at harbor, sailors feared they knew that the ship was going to sink at sea.

Jonahs: A Jonah was a person or thing aboard ship that brought bad luck. This superstition comes from a biblical story where Jonah was punished by God because he boarded a ship and fled his duty to preach. The ship was plagued by storms until the crew cast lots and threw Jonah overboard. It was only then that the seas became calm.

Anyone dressed in black: Sailors especially feared the clergy because of their association with the sick and the dead. They believed pious men would attract the wrath of the devil, who would punish them with storms.

24

Birds: Killing a bird that followed a ship at sea, usually a gull, stormy petrel, or albatross, was considered a bad omen.

Cats: Cats were believed to bring on bad weather. Despite this, they were common pets onboard.

Dead bodies: A dead body aboard ship was seen as a sign of coming disaster. If a man died while at sea, his body was placed in a canvas sack, which was sewn shut and released into the ocean.

Sharks: Sailors hated sharks. If a shark followed a ship with a sick person aboard, it foretold that person's death.

Clothes: Wearing the clothes of a sailor who died at sea before the voyage was over was considered bad luck.

Children: Children onboard were a sign of good luck.

Women: Women as bad luck aboard ship was a common superstition, but in reality sailors welcomed a voyage where the captain's wife was aboard. Her presence sometimes softened shipboard punishment and reminded the sailors of home.

Mop or bucket overboard: Losing a mop or a bucket overboard was a sign of bad things to come.

Modern Superstitions

Changing a boat's name: This is considered extremely bad luck.

Shoes upside down on deck: This is bad luck because an overturned shoe resembles a capsized boat.

Coins: Coins under a ship's mast will bring good winds.

Dolphins: These friendly creatures are a sign of good luck.

Blessing of the fleet: A member of the clergy blesses a ship to bring good weather and a safe voyage.

Breaking a bottle of champagne on the bow of a ship: It christens the ship with good luck on its launching.

(The answer to the spelled out code on page 23 is "CREW CUT.")

Make a Sailor's Tattoo

Life on a ship was dangerous. A tattoo was a practical form of identification for a sailor. Because many men died at sea, it was sometimes the only way a body could be recognized. Tattoos were permanent and personal. They couldn't be stolen, borrowed, or destroyed.

American sailors first became interested in the art of tattooing when they encountered the natives of the South Pacific. The natives tattooed elaborate designs for them, which they copied with images of their own aboard ship. Before long, the better shipboard artists opened up parlors in seaport towns, and the practice became an art associated with sailors. It became nearly impossible to find a sailor in the 19th century who didn't sport at least one tattoo.

Here are some tattoo images and their meanings.

Crucifix: Catholic sailors had the crucifix tattooed on their chests to ensure that they would receive last rites and burial according to their faith. Sailors of all faiths often had the crucifix tattooed on both feet as a protection against sharks.

A pig tattooed on one foot, and a rooster on the other: These symbols were thought to offer protection from drowning.

"HARD LUCK" tattooed across the knuckles: This phrase, ironically enough, was thought to bring its wearer good luck.

Anchor: This icon meant that the sailor had sailed the Atlantic Ocean.

Full-rigged ship: This tattoo served as evidence that the sailor had sailed around Cape Horn.

Shellback turtle: This illustration informed others that the sailor had crossed the equator.

The words *HOLD* on one hand and *FAST* on the other: This was supposed to help the sailor hold on to the rigging.

Flags and eagles: These icons symbolized patriotism.

Ship: This tattoo proclaimed the wearer's pride at being a sailor.

Hearts and flowers: These were merely body decoration.

Here's how you can make your own tattoo that isn't permanent.

What You Need

Thick layer of newspaper
1 tablespoon plus 2 teaspoons (10 milliliters) cornstarch
1 tablespoon (15 milliliters) water
1 tablespoon (15 milliliters) face cream/moisturizer
Mixing spoon
Small bowl
Empty egg carton or 3 small cups
Food coloring
3 plastic spoons
Paintbrush

What You Do

1. Spread out newspapers in your work space.
2. Using the spoon, mix the cornstarch, water, and face cream in the bowl.
3. Divide the mixture into three sections of the egg carton or into the cups.
4. Add several drops of a different color food coloring into each section and mix well with a different spoon.
5. Paint a tattoo from the designs below or think up your own. The tattoo will wash off easily with soap and water.

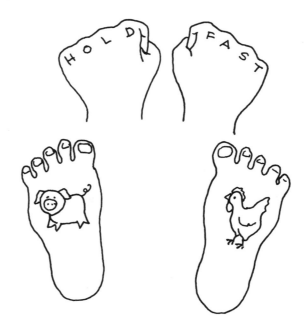

Be a Lookout

All sailors had to stand watch on deck as lookouts. They watched for signs of danger: ships sailing too close, icebergs and rocks, approaching storms, and land that they had to navigate toward or avoid. The lives of the sailors and the safety of the ship depended on the lookout.

For whalemen, the lookout was extremely important because their livelihood depended on the sighting of whales. Lookouts on a *whaler* (a whaling vessel) stood on *mastheads* (the tops of masts) 100 or more feet (30.48 or more meters) above deck to get the most panoramic view of the ocean. They had to be keenly aware of the smallest movements and sounds.

Try standing lookout in your neighborhood. You will be amazed at all the things that go on there.

What You Need

Watch
Notebook
Pen or pencil

What You Do

1. Sit in a central location on your block such as on a front porch or street corner.
2. Listen and watch for all the sights, sounds, and smells around you for 20 minutes and record them in the notebook. Here are some observations to consider.
   - Do you see a bird? Where? What color is it?
   - Is there a train whistle? A plane flying overhead? From what direction?
   - What is the weather like? Is the wind light, moderate, or brisk?
   - Is it sunny? Cloudy? Rainy?
   - How many people pass by? Do they see you? Do they say anything to you?
   - Do you see any animals such as a dog, cat, squirrel, or rabbit?
   - Are there mosquitoes or bees buzzing?
   - What do you smell? Freshly cut lawn? Dinner cooking? Is there smoke coming out of a chimney? An aroma of food cooking?
3. After you're finished with your 20 minutes of observation, go inside and write a story that uses all of the elements you observed.

Shipboard Discipline

Discipline aboard ship was often swift and severe. The captain was the father, ruler, and master at sea, and the lowly sailor had little recourse against his wrath. Of course as in all occupations there were kindly and fair captains, but even these men did not hesitate to order a flogging or a beating with a *belaying pin* (a wooden pin used to secure lines) if they thought the safety of the ship was at stake.

Until shipboard floggings were outlawed in 1850, breaking a rule at sea typically resulted in a certain number of lashes from a cat-o'-nine-tails. The crew was ordered on deck to witness the punishment. The officers hoped that watching the punishment would deter further misbehavior from the sailors. The "cat," made out of knotted leather rope, was a cruel instrument of torture that inflicted deep, bleeding wounds. After a flogging, a sailor suffered for days in constant pain and unable to sleep, but he was still expected to work.

Putting a man in leg and wrist irons (also known as shackles) was the preferred method of punishment once flogging was outlawed. It was a way to subdue and humiliate a rebellious sailor. Many captains routinely kicked, pushed, and punched sailors to keep them submissive. Strong-willed men who spoke back to an officer were subjected to longer, slower forms of punishment, such as confinement in a locker (a small storage space in the *hold*, or bottom of the ship), a *trypot* (a large cooking vessel used to boil blubber into oil), or a *cask* (see page 8), or were kept below decks in irons. Captains might also punish sailors by denying their basic human needs such as food, drink, or sleep.

A passive way for a man to rebel was to pretend to be sick. Suspected fakers were called *sogers*. The soger might succeed in getting out of some chores, but often what passed for medical care was worse than working. The captain, who also acted as the ship's doctor, prescribed treatment according to 19th-century methods like bleeding, blistering, purging, and vomiting. Sometimes sick sailors got better, but often they got worse. People were unaware of the existence of germs such as viruses and bacteria, which we now know cause most forms of illness.

Another way sailors rebelled was to let a whale get away on purpose. It hurt the captain far more than the crew financially, and it was sometimes worth it to get back at a cruel skipper.

The ultimate justice for a sailor with a grudge was to circulate gossip at home. If a captain had been fair and just, even if he led with a firm hand, then the talk would be complimentary. If he had been cruel and unfair, the sailors could ruin his reputation among sailors and townspeople. A shrewd ship owner stayed clear of unpopular captains for fear of mutiny and loss of income. If the captain's "character," or reputation, was damaged, his career was all but over.

Animals Onboard

Cats and dogs did not like being onboard ship. Dogs barked incessantly and had nowhere to run and play in the tight quarters. Cats hated the tipping decks and the wet spray from the ocean. Despite these problems, kittens and puppies were often given as gifts to children and women aboard.

Sailors enjoyed bringing home unusual pets from the various foreign ports they visited. Monkeys, parrots, and cockatoos were popular. A trip to Honolulu, where hogs were plentiful, usually culminated in a bounty of them sliding back and forth across the deck as the ship pitched and rolled. In the Galápagos Islands, whalemen captured giant tortoises. These animals could live for up to a year without food or water, they yielded delicious meat when slaughtered, and they provided rides for the captain's children.

Mice, rats, cockroaches, and weevils were the uninvited guests onboard. They contaminated food supplies and spread disease. Sailors shot at the rats with guns, and they trained dogs and cats to hunt down mice and rats. They set traps and fumigated the ship. Despite these measures, pests were always a problem.

When ships traveled to exotic destinations, shipmasters enjoyed the attention they received from bringing back an animal never seen by Americans. New England ships brought back an African lion, a camel, and Arabian stallions. In 1817, Captain Crowninshield from Salem, Massachusetts, brought the first elephant to America. It sold for $10,000 on the dock!

Sailors often named things aboard ship after animals. The *crow's nest* was the lookout's platform at the top of the mast, called a *hogshead*, a *donkey's breakfast* was a mattress filled with straw, *dogwatches* were the half watches at dinnertime, and a *catwalk* was a narrow passageway.

Make a Sea Chest

The *sea chest* represented the little privacy a sailor had onboard ship. In it, he kept his tobacco, clothes, tools, *ditty box* (see page 48), hat, letters from home, and maybe a Bible or some other book. It served both as a chair and a table in the crowded fo'c'sle. Sea chests were made of wood and were about three feet by one foot (about 91 by 30 centimeters) long with hinged flat covers. They were typically painted green, gray, or blue. The inside lid was where the decoration was done, as if to emphasize that it was a private space. The artwork usually included symbols of the sea: anchors, compasses, whales, stars, ropes, and knots. Countless hours were put into the fancy beckets (rope handles) that were placed at the sides of the chest. Sailors traditionally made their own sea chests, but they could also be purchased from skilled craftsmen.

What You Need

Heavy cardboard box with a lid (such as a produce box from the grocery store)

Scissors

Paintbrush

Acrylic paint in gray, blue, or green

Compass or round plate to make a circle

Medium-point black marker

Wide duct tape

Paper

Pen

What You Do

1. Cut one long side of the box's lid off so it can be hinged with tape to the box.
2. Paint the outside of the box and lid. You will probably need two coats. Let them dry.
3. On the inside of the lid, use the compass or plate to draw a large circle, and fill it in with the marker to make a compass as shown.
4. Hinge the lid and box together with the tape.
5. Imagine you are going on a voyage of a year or longer. What would you need to take? Place as many of the items as will fit into your box, and list all the rest on a sheet of paper that you place in the box, too.

Ship's chest and contents. *Peabody Essex Museum*

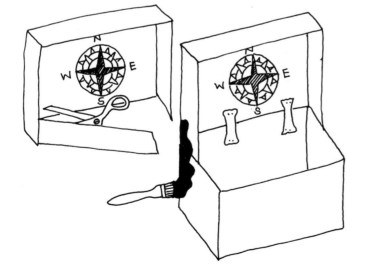

Collect Fresh Rainwater

Fresh water was carefully preserved aboard ship, because ocean water is deadly to drink. The reason is that ocean water has about four times as much salt as you have in your blood. If you were to drink seawater, the concentration of salt in your blood would rise. This would tell your kidneys that they need to flush out all that extra salt. The only problem is that the kidneys use up a lot of water when they flush out salt! The end result is that you would be *more* thirsty and *more* dehydrated than if you'd drunk nothing.

The scarcity of fresh water affected much more than what sailors drank, however. Those of us on land don't realize how much fresh water we use each day. If sailors used the same amount, their supplies would be drastically diminished in a day.

Water onboard was kept in tanks and casks. Rats often crawled inside tanks and drowned, contaminating the water. Wooden casks of water grew bacteria after sitting in the warm hold of the ship for months, and sometimes the wood of the cask broke down and affected the water's quality. Casks often were used over and over again, and the previous contents of the cask spoiled the new water.

Drinking water soon became foul and slimy, so it was only drunk if mixed with rum or beer, or boiled for coffee or tea. Pots, pans, and cooking utensils were scrubbed with sand and rinsed in salt water. Clothes at sea became incredibly filthy, especially for whalemen. The men used seawater, ashes, and often urine to clean their clothes and then towed the clothes on a line in the ocean for two or three days.

We're not sure why ashes and urine worked as a detergent to clean whale oil, but a guess is that urine would cut through the whale oil like vinegar. The ashes probably worked to absorb some of the oil, as would powder. Why do *you* think they would use these substances to clean clothes?

Bathing, as we know it, was infrequent. However, seagoing children remember taking cold saltwater baths on deck in a makeshift bathtub. They probably were bathed more often because they were smaller and required less water.

When it rained, sailors collected fresh rainwater by stopping up the *scuppers* (deck drains) and putting out buckets. This was particularly delightful in the tropics where it was warm and the men stripped down to wash themselves and their clothes. They hung their laundry from the rigging and let it dry in the sun. A cold Atlantic rain, however, was not as welcome. Clothes and bedding might stay damp and cold for days afterward.

What You Need

Buckets, pots, and pans
Rain shower
Ruler

What You Do

1. To see how difficult it was for sailors to collect a quantity of rainwater aboard ship, put two or three containers outside next time it rains.
2. When the rain shower is over, use the ruler to measure how many inches you have. Try washing a load of clothes using only this amount of water. Is it enough? Think of other ways to clean clothes if you only had this much water aboard ship.

Heave Ho! Make a Ship's Anchor

A tall ship, depending on its size, might carry five or more anchors. The two main anchors, or bower anchors, were carried on either side of the bow, or front, of the ship. Other anchors that ships carried were a sheet anchor as a spare in case something happened to one of the main anchors; a kedge anchor to use when moving the ship; a lightweight stream anchor, about half the weight of a main anchor, used for low tide or shallow water; and a grapnel anchor, a small, pronged anchor that could be used to drag the ocean bottom to find lost objects.

Lifting an enormous anchor was a grueling task for sailors. It could take as long as four hours to lift each one and they weighed as much as 3,000 pounds (1.36 metric tons)! The anchors had to be brought up one at a time using a mechanical winch called the *capstan*. Sailors inserted long wooden bars, known as handspikes, into the capstan. This looked like a giant wagon wheel without a rim, lying sideways across a barrel-like foundation, the handspikes sticking out like long spokes. Two or three men held onto each handspike as they pushed it around. They usually sang a sea chantey such as the one below as they lifted the anchor.

Rio Grand
(capstan chantey)

Were you ever in Rio Grand? Way Rio
Oh were you ever on that strand
We're bound for the Rio Grand
Way Rio, way Rio
Then fare you well, my pretty young girl
We're bound for the Rio Grand

Where the Portugee girls can be found, way Rio
And they are the girls to waltz around
We're bound for the Rio Grand

Way Rio, way Rio
Then fare you well, my pretty young girl
We're bound for the Rio Grand

What You Need

A grown-up to assist
2 or 3 newspapers or 1 thick Sunday newspaper
Masking or clear tape
Scissors

What You Do

1. To make the shank (the stem of the anchor), take four pages of newspaper and roll them up loosely the long way into a 2- to 3-inch (5.08- to 7.62-centimeter) tube.
2. Make another tube the same way and tuck its end into the end of the first tube.
3. Tape together.
4. Continue making and connecting tubes until you've got one tube about 10 feet (3.05 meters) long.
5. To make the stock (the cross piece of the anchor), roll up another tube.
6. Ask an adult to cut a hole through the shank about 1 foot (30.48 centimeters) down, large enough to slip the stock tube through, but not so large that the shank tube splits into two.

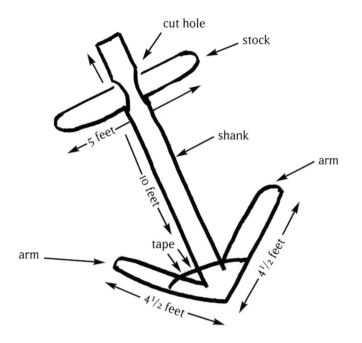

7. Make more tubes, attaching them to each side of the stock tube. This should end up to be about 5 feet (1.52 meters) long.
8. To make the *arms* (the extensions that branch out from the bottom of the shank), make two more tubes, taping each one to the bottom of the shank slanting, upward to make a giant *V*.
9. Continue making tubes and attaching them to the arms until each is about 4.5 feet (1.37 meters) long.

When you're finished, lift your anchor while imagining it weighs 3,000 pounds (1.36 metric tons). How many people would you need to lift it?

Create a Squeezebox

At the end of a long day, usually during the second dogwatch (from 6 to 8 P.M.), the sailors took time to relax and enjoy themselves. Singing, dancing, and making music were popular pastimes in the fo'c'sle. There was usually a sailor with a squeezebox and a man or two willing to stomp out a song.

The term *squeezebox* is an informal name for a small accordion or concertina—free-reed instruments. The concertina was invented by Sir Charles Wheatstone in 1829. Wheatstone concertinas were made for more than 100 years. A Wheatstone concertina can be identified by a wheat design on the handles.

You make these instruments work by pressing handles on either side of a rectangular *bellows* (pleated airbag) in and out, to pump air to the *reeds* (flexible strips of metal). You produce the sound you want when you press the keys or buttons.

Squeezeboxes were made of many combinations of material: wood, metal, leather, paper, and various textiles. Many were painted black or red, and often the handles were adorned with ornamental *fretwork* (three-dimensional openwork, or decoration).

What You Need

Ruler
22-inch (55.88-centimeter) by 28-inch (71.12-centimeter) poster board, either red or black
Scissors (large and small)
Stapler
Piece of silver or gray construction paper
Pencil
Glue stick
Hole punch
4 brass fasteners
Circular object to trace, smaller than a dime
Small piece of black or white felt
Music box disk (These are little buttons you sometimes see inside birthday cards that play a simple song when pressed, available in craft stores.)
Square of poster board tape

What You Do

1. Measure and cut out a 7-inch (17.78-centimeter) strip from the long side of the poster board.
2. Now cut another 7-inch (17.78-centimeter) strip from the board.
3. Fold each piece every 4 inches (10.16-centimeter), accordion style, until you get to the end. One end of each piece will be short.
4. Staple the two strips together in the middle, leaving the short ends on either side.
5. Cut out two strips of the silver or gray construction paper, 2½ inches (6.35 centimeters) by 5 inches (12.7 centimeters).
6. With the pencil draw ornamental designs on each strip.
7. Use the small scissors to cut the middle of the design out, so that the design is in the openwork, meaning you can see through it.
8. Glue over each end of the squeezebox as fretwork.
9. To make handles, cut two 5-inch (12.7-centimeter) by ½-inch (1.27-centimeter) strips from the remaining poster board.
10. Punch a hole at either end of each strip. Then punch two holes ½-inch (1.27-centimeter) from each end of the accordion and about 3 inches (7.62 centimeters) apart.
11. Attach the handles to the accordion by tucking each end under. It should look something like a suitcase handle.
12. Push a fastener through one hole in a handle and then through the hole in the end of the accordion. Flip the accordian upside down and open the prongs to secure the handle end. Now do the same to the other three handle ends.
13. Trace several small circles on the felt and cut out.
14. Paste the circles onto the sides of the squeezebox to look like buttons. In the inside corner of the last fold, tape the music box disk to the accordion with the poster tape square.

Now you can play the squeezebox by slipping four fingers on each hand under the handles, and pressing the disk with your thumb to start the music. Pull the squeezebox in and out and press the felt buttons as the music plays.

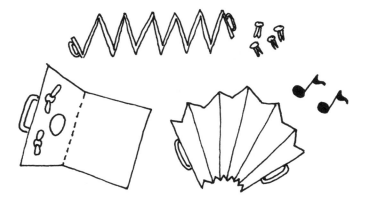

Dance the Sailor's Hornpipe

The hornpipe is an old dance from England that was a favorite among seafarers. Accompanied by the music of the *hornpipe*, a type of tin flute, this solo dance was performed barefoot on deck. The movements mimic the sailor's work: hoisting sails, climbing rigging, rowing a boat, and standing lookout.

Here is a simple version of the sailor's hornpipe.

What You Need

Large space to dance

One or more people

Music such as "The Sailor's Hornpipe" or another sea song (There are a lot of sea songs and chanteys on CDs and tapes you can borrow from your local library.)

What You Do

Form a circle with the other dancers. You will follow each other as you dance. There is a toe step and a heel step. Learn these two steps before you add the hand motions.

Toe step: Making a hopping motion, first land your left foot and tap your right toe in front of it, then land your right foot and tap your left toe in front of it. Always do the step to a count of eight.

Heel step: Making a hopping motion, first land your left foot and tap your right heel in front of it, then land your right foot and tap your left heel in front of it. Always do the step to a count of eight.

Now you can add the hand motions. At the beginning of each hand motion the movement will indicate the step you should be doing.

Movement 1: Toe step to a count of eight while keeping your arms crossed over your chest.

Movement 2: Heel step to a count of eight while placing your right hand across the front of your waist and the left hand on the small of your back.

Movement 3: Toe step to a count of eight while acting as if you were pulling down on a rope to adjust a sail.

Movement 4: Heel step to a count of eight while pretending you are climbing the rigging (a rope ladder).

Movement 5: Toe step to a count of eight while pulling your hands into your chest and out as if you were rowing a boat.

Movement 6: Heel step to a count of eight while acting as if you are standing lookout by shading one eye with your hand.

Movement 7: Toe step to a count of eight while pretending you are pulling up on a rope as if lifting an anchor.

Salute to finish.

Cooking in a Rolling Kitchen: The Ship's Cook

The cook and the crew had an odd relationship. Although the crew was at the cook's mercy at mealtime, they often treated him poorly. He was blamed for serving spoiled food or small portions even though it was actually the captain and mates who were responsible for what the sailors received. Cooking was seen at that time as women's work, meaning it did not require great strength or daring. Officers considered cooking to be unimportant, and they usually gave the job to the youngest or least experienced hand. Or it would be given to a man who had lost a leg or was otherwise physically unable to perform sailors' duties. In later years, many cooks were black or Asian, which was largely the result of shipboard discrimination. The cook's nickname was usually "Doc." According to historical accounts, this term was meant to both honor and mock (make fun of) him.

Here are the things you'd find in a typical ship's galley:

Cast-iron stove
Pots, pans, and kettles
Steamer
Pie plates
Graters
Teakettle
Coffeepot
Carving forks and knives
Tin cups, forks, and spoons
Ladles
Cooking spoons
Dippers
Bake pans
Pudding bags
Colanders
Funnel
Chopping tray

The cook was a part of the crew known as the *idlers*, crew members who were specialists in one area. Idlers worked through daylight hours and slept through the night. They were not part of the watch system. The other idlers were the carpenter, the sail-maker (see page 169), the cooper (see page 172), and the steward.

Doc was responsible for cooking, keeping the galley clean, and cleaning the copper or iron pots and pans known as coppers. He did have other duties aboard ship: he was in charge of the foresail when the ship was changing tack (changing direction) and he had specific tasks *aloft* (up in the rigging).

Richard Henry Dana expressed a favorable view of the cook's role in the nonfiction book *Two Years Before the Mast*: "The cook is the patron of the crew, and those in his favor can get their wet mittens and stockings dried, or light their pipes at the galley on their night watch." The cook was the one who decided if the men would be allowed to use the stove to make a snack such as dandyfunk.

Cooking aboard ship involved mostly cutting and boiling. It was not a skilled profession, but as the ship pitched and rolled, the pots and pans filled with hot food rolled with it. It must have taken good balance to keep from losing food or getting burned during the cooking process!

Slush Fund

If he wanted to, the cook could skimp on cooking ingredients such as fat. This was an important source of calories for hardworking men. It also added flavor to the food. The excess fat or grease, called slush, was collected and sold to soap manufacturers at the end of the voyage, and the cook received a percentage of the money. This was known as the slush fund and it was used to buy small luxuries for the crew. Now the term *slush fund* means "money used for illegal purposes such as bribes or buying votes in an election."

Cook Bean Soup

An ordinary dinner for sailors was hardtack, salted meat, and bean soup. A staple of the fo'c'sle, bean soup was warm and filling after a long day at sea. The cook let it simmer until the beans were the consistency of oatmeal. Try this recipe. If you want to eat the soup the way the sailors did, mash it with a potato masher when it's done.

What You Need

A grown-up to assist
2 cups (453 grams) dry navy beans
Large bowl
Frying pan (nonstick preferred)
4 thick bacon slices
Large spoon
Paper towels
Paring knife
Potato peeler

1 large onion
2 large potatoes
8 ounces (227 grams) pre-peeled baby carrots
Cutting board
Colander
Slow cooker or crockpot
5 cups (1.18 liters) water
2 teaspoons (6 grams) salt
½ teaspoon (1.5 grams) freshly ground black pepper
½ teaspoon (1.5 grams) red pepper (cayenne)
Potato masher (optional)

What You Do

1. Soak the beans overnight in a bowl of water.
2. With the supervision of an adult, fry the bacon over medium heat until crisp.
3. Using a large spoon, transfer the bacon to paper towels, leaving the drippings in the pan.

4. Have an adult remove the skin from the onion, and peel the potatoes with the potato peeler.

5. Work together to chop the onion, potatoes, and carrots into bite-size pieces.

6. Fry the onion in the leftover bacon drippings.

7. Drain the navy beans in the colander and discard the soaking water.

8. Crumble the bacon slices.

9. Put all the ingredients, including the water and spices, in the slow cooker.

10. Cook on low for 10 to 12 hours. You do not need to stir.

Yield: 6 large servings

Gamming: A Shipboard Party!

A *gam*, or shipboard party held when two ships met at sea, was a pleasant diversion from the tedium and hard work of shipboard life. It was especially loved by whalemen during long voyages. Merchant ships carrying cargo had a specific destination and the crew wanted to get there quickly. Whalers, on the other hand, were in no rush once they got to the whaling grounds. Their mission was to wait for whales, and the time could pass very slowly.

Though they were competing in the same business, there was a fellowship among whalers. A fellow whaling ship was always pleasantly greeted. During a gam, a ship would anchor alongside another ship for a day or two. The crew was eager to socialize and visit new surroundings. Living on a whaler for months on end was like being stuck in the house. The captain on one ship selected as many as half a watch of his men to row over to the other ship. Then the other ship's first mate and the same number of men would visit the first ship. If the gam went on for several hours or days, the men would circulate in groups back and forth until each sailor had the opportunity to visit the other ship.

Wives and children aboard ships particularly looked forward to gams. Living on an all-male ship, they might not see other women and children for a year or more. A special chair called a gamming chair was lowered over the side of the ship so the captain's wife would not have to climb a rope ladder. Women exchanged homemade treats of preserves and nuts, favorite books, and small animals such as kittens and birds. They admired each other's embroidery and drank tea from fine china cups. The children played hide and seek and tag, swapped toys, and sneaked into forbidden areas of the ship.

Captains enjoyed gams just as much as the crew did. The strict social divisions onboard ship did not allow for socializing with the crew. Captains lived, ate, and generally worked in separate quarters from the men in the fo'c'sle. It was somewhat like the military, where the safety of the ship depends on the sailors obeying orders. Even if it was isolating, the captain had to maintain a position of authority over his crew. During a gam he could relax and enjoy a laugh and a drink with the other captain. They shared notes about position, weather, and whale sightings.

If a whale was sighted during a gam, the two ships would hunt it together and then split the profits. This practice was known as *mating*.

Sailors delivered mail, traded tobacco and handiwork, and shared the latest gossip with the crew of the other ship. Long fanciful tales were spun about the whales they had slain, cannibals they had encountered, storms they had survived, and beautiful women they had left behind. They grumbled about their captains, shared food and grog (watered-down rum), sang and danced, and longed for home.

Make a Ditty Box

A sailor's *ditty box* held small personal items such as shaving tools, combs, and letters from home, as well as several sailmaking tools: needles, thimbles, a sewing palm (see page 94), an awl for making holes, and fids for splicing rope. Sailors thought of it as a sewing box as opposed to the sea chest, which held clothes, books, and other larger items. Ditty boxes were round, rectangular, or square and were usually made from wood on a merchant ship or whalebone on a whaler. The cover was often adorned with *scrimshaw* (inked whalebone carvings), wood etchings (designs carved into the wood), or paintings.

What You Need

Layer of newspaper

Round papier-mâché box with lid (available in craft stores)

Brown acrylic paint (to look like wood) or ivory acrylic paint (to look like whalebone)

Paintbrush

Scissors

Nautical pictures from magazines, coloring books, newspapers, or wrapping paper featuring anchors, eagles, compasses, clipper ships, ships' wheels, whales, stars, or flags

Satin decoupage medium (a combination water-based
    sealer, glue, and finish available in craft stores)
Napkin

What You Do

1. Place a layer of newspaper over your work area.
2. Paint the box and lid with the acrylic paint. Let dry.
3. Cut out pictures.
4. Glue the pictures down on the lid and sides with the
   decoupage medium.
5. Press to get all the bubbles out.
6. Dab the excess with the napkin. Let dry.
7. Paint a thin layer of decoupage medium over the
   entire box and lid. Let dry.
8. Add more layers if desired.

King Neptune's Visit

ear! That's what the greenhands felt when it was time to "cross the line," or pass over the equator. They knew as the ship approached the 0° latitude at the equator that they would be put through an old-time initiation rite known as King Neptune's Visit. Originally the ancient ritual was to appease the god of water, Neptune, and bring the ship good luck. During the days of the tall ships it evolved into a ceremony that the greenhands had to pass through before being welcomed into the brotherhood of sailors. The crew, not the officers, orchestrated the visit and in a not-too-gentle manner. Sailors who had gone through it themselves found great pleasure in teasing and tormenting the new recruits.

On the day of the crossing, the greenhands were kept below decks until one of the crew, dressed as King Neptune, appeared. The crew beat tin pans, pots, cans, and whatever else they could find to announce his majesty's arrival. Dressed in a robe and with a crown and trident, King Neptune wore a costume that was a hodge-podge of whatever was onboard. Typically the robe was a blanket secured with a rope. The king wore large sea boots, whiskers, and seaweed made from rope-yarn. He also had a *speaking trumpet* (a metal trumpet-shaped instrument that the captain used for calling out to other ships) and a tool such as a porpoise fork for a trident.

The greenhands were blindfolded and led one by one from the fo'c'stle to the deck to sit on a plank over a tub of water. Interrogated by King Neptune, they were called names such as soger and *lubber*, meaning "clumsy sailor," and asked a series of silly questions. The members of the king's court varied from ship to ship depending on the size of the crew. On a small ship there was only King Neptune, ruler of the sea, but on larger ships the crew might include his wife, Queen

Amphitrite; Triton with his trumpet; Davy Jones with horns and tail as the court jester; and a sea lawyer who was supposed to defend the recruits but instead created further problems for them.

The greenhand was asked his name, age, and land of origin, as well as several nonsense questions. As he answered, a swab was shoved into his mouth covered with tar and grease. He was asked to swear to uphold the laws of the sea, and then lathered with a mixture of tar and grease and shaved with a wooden razor, or worse, a rusty barrel hoop. He was then welcomed as a son of Neptune and led to believe that the ceremony was over.

At this point the crew pulled the plank underneath him, dunking him into the tub of cold saltwater. The ritual concluded when they removed his blindfold and he shook hands with King Neptune. No matter what his age, the greenhand was thereafter referred to as an old salt. He was then granted the privilege of watching the next interrogation. There would be a round of grog or ale for all and gingerbread at supper.

Perform a Play About King Neptune's Visit

This is a fun play modeled after the ritual of King Neptune's Visit (without the tar and grease of course). Look through your closets for costumes using whatever's available, just as the sailors did.

What You Need

Characters

One or more greenhands

King Neptune

Members of his court, as many as you wish, including Queen Amphitrite, Triton, Davy Jones, and the sea lawyer

Costume Suggestions

King Neptune: Bathrobe, blanket, or sheet for a robe; rope or belt to tie around the waist; any type of boots; dress-up crown or hat; fake beard and wig; broom or other tool to use as a trident; and paper towel roll for a speaking trumpet

Greenhands: Jeans, striped shirt, and scarf tied around the neck

Queen Amphitrite: Long gown or sheet for dress

Davy Jones: Devil costume

Triton: Robe, blanket, or sheet for robe and paper towel roll for trumpet

Sea lawyer: Robe, sheet, or blanket for robe

Props

Pots, pans, and spoons to announce King Neptune's visit

Scarf to blindfold the greenhands

Chair for the greenhand to sit on while being interrogated

Small paper cup filled halfway with water for the dunking

Ginger ale

Cups for the celebration

What You Do

1. The greenhands are held in the fo'c'sle, which could be a small room or the space under a table. The court arrives, beating pots and pans to announce King Neptune.

2. One by one the greenhands are led blindfolded from the fo'c'sle to the main deck (a room with a chair) for the ceremony. The greenhand is asked to sit down. King Neptune then asks the following questions:

   What is ye last name spelled backward?
   How old are ye?
   Where were ye born?
   Is a mermaid a fish or a woman?
   What does Davy Jones keep in his locker?
   Do ye promise always to collect seaweed with your
      toes as ye walk along the beach?

   Think up some more silly questions of your own.

3. Welcome the new recruit as a son or daughter of Neptune. Then, when the new recruit least expects it, pour the water over his or her head! Once you do this, you cannot ask the greenhand any more questions.

4. Take off the blindfold, shake hands, and welcome the greenhand as an old salt. Each new son or daughter of Neptune gets to watch the interrogation of the next greenhand. When everyone is finished, toast the new old salts with ginger ale.

"Crossing the Line" from the journal of Edward Haskell aboard the *Tarquin*, 1862. *Peabody Essex Museum*

Speaking a Ship

When another ship was sighted at sea, the custom was to "speak it." Speaking a ship was a formal interchange, even if the two captains were old friends. Each captain stood on deck with a speaking trumpet. He was careful to avoid holding onto anything in order to show his *sea legs* (show that he could stand upright on deck even when it pitched with the waves).

Ship 1: "What ship is that?"
Ship 2: "The *Hannah Jones* from Salem."
Ship 1: "Where are you bound?"
Ship 2: "Canton."
Ship 1: "How many days out?"
Ship 2: "One hundred and five."

Then the conversation was reversed, with the answering captain now asking the questions.

Finally each ship displayed a large blackboard with the latitude and longitude marked on it, so that they could compare figures for accuracy. If they were not in pursuit of whales, the interchange often concluded with a gam (see page 46).

In the next chapter we will learn what it was like to work aboard a whaling ship. The job of a whaleman was dirty as well as dangerous. The men had to be skilled in both the difficult work of the sailor and the dangerous job of the whaleman.

2

There She Blows! The Whalers

Join us and learn about the hunt for the whale: the harpooner making his mark, the chase, the slaughter, and finally the boiling of the blubber into whalemen's gold—whale oil. Discover the types of whales that were hunted and why, shiver as you hear the tragic story of the whaleship *Essex*, and make your own whaleboat and gear. Imagine being onboard a whaler trapped in the Arctic in 1871. Then try your hand at making an iceberg that floats. Finally, carve a piece of scrimshaw and enjoy a hot slice of plum duff—the whalemen's favorite treat.

The Fantasy Versus the Reality of Life Aboard a Whaler

A young man living in a seaport town such as New Bedford, Massachusetts, grew up hearing *yarns* (sailors' stories) about life aboard a whaler. The old salts would spin tales of conquering the mighty whale, sailing through storm-whipped seas, and exploring exotic ports in the Pacific Islands. To young men this was the pinnacle of bravery and masculinity. They were eager to join this brotherhood that included their own fathers, uncles, cousins, and friends. Many were farmers lured to the whaling life by colorful advertisements that glamorized the adventure and independence of deepwater sailing.

The reality was much different. Life aboard a whaler was difficult and dangerous. The young sailors were often treated harshly, fed poorly, and underpaid. Instead of a salary, whalemen received a *lay*, a portion of how much money was made from the the total catch of whales. The captain might receive ¹⁄₁₀ of a lay, but a common seaman could look forward to only about ¹⁄₁₅₀ or less. If prices for whale oil or *baleen* (whale cartilage) dropped, or if whales were scarce, it was the common whaleman who suffered the losses. It was not unusual to hear that a man had earned nothing after a three- or four-year voyage! Worse yet, he could even owe money because of the high prices he had to pay when buying from the *slop chest*, which was a type of ship's store for the desperate. The ship sold clothes, tobacco, knives, needles, thread, and other things sailors would need over the course of the voyage. The slop chest's proprietors charged twice as much as the poor sailor would have paid at home.

The whaling ship was filled with young men from all parts of the world seeking a better life. In addition to native-born New Englanders, the crews often included a good number of blacks and Native Americans, Cape Verdeans, Samoans, Fiji Islanders, Azoreans, and Kanakas from Hawaii.

A Whaling Ship's Hierarchy

The whaleman's position aboard ship determined where he bunked and what he ate. The fo'c'sle, located at the very front of the ship, was the living quarters for the common sailors. This triangular space followed the shape of the ship and was where about 25 men lived and slept for the three to four years of a typical whaling expedition. The only light that was able to filter in came from a small hatchway cut in the deck that allowed the men to climb in and out. It was almost unbearably stuffy and dark in the fo'c'sle, especially when the hatch was closed for bad weather. Each man was assigned a bunk built into the side of the ship and allowed only enough space to place his sea chest on the floor. In the first days of the voyage, the fo'c'sle reeked of vomit and tobacco. The young men groaned in their bunks as cockroaches and rats ran underfoot.

The next level after the common seamen were the skilled sailors, whose quarters were in midship, known as the *steerage*. On one side there was a stateroom for the harpooners, and on the other side the blacksmith, carpenter, cooper (see page 172), steward, and cook shared quarters.

The officers were in the *stern*, or back, of the ship. They included the first mate, a man responsible for many important things, such as making sure the captain's orders were followed and supervising the work, including maintenance and repair of the ship's *standing rigging* (the fixed lines that secure the yards and masts in place) and *running rigging* (the lines that adjust the sails). It was also up to the first mate to oversee the deck crew in their chores (see page 92) and during the hunting and processing of whales; make entries in the logbook; and safeguard the cargo. The position of the second mate was not an enviable one. He was not granted the respect given to the first mate because he was expected to perform ordinary sailor's duties along with the men. He had to relay the first mate's orders and manage the rope locker. The only duty he was exempted from was standing watch at the helm. Larger ships had third or even fourth mates who shared these responsibilities.

The cabin boy, whose job was to wait on the officers, also bunked in the stern. The mates and cabin boy had the special privilege of eating in the main cabin with the captain, where they sat at a table and were served by the steward. The men in steerage ate after the officers in the main cabin.

The captain was the only one onboard who had his own quarters. He had a bed, a chest of drawers, a medicine chest, and usually a couch as well. Some captains had a bed hung with gimbals (a system of hinges) that kept the bed level as the ship pitched over the waves. If his wife and children were aboard, they shared his quarters.

The captain of a whaling ship enjoyed the best quarters but also shouldered the most responsibility. The lives of the entire crew depended on him. He had to encourage the men to work hard, bring in a good catch of whales, keep the ship in working order, ride out violent storms, discipline unruly men, doctor the sick, navigate the course, and ultimately bring back a full shipment of whale oil.

First Days on the Job

Within hours of shipping out, the greenhand would feel the first pangs of seasickness. As the ship pitched and rolled with the waves, there was nothing to fix the eyes on but sky and sea. The first days were an agonizing trial of learning to climb rigging, hoist sails, sharpen tools, practice whaleboat drills, and clean the ship. But instead of having compassion, the old salts delighted in seeing the greenhands struggle. They teased them mercilessly and expected them to do their share of the work, sick or not.

After a few miserable days the greenie's seasickness subsided. He managed to find his sea legs by adopting the rolling walk of the sailor. Gradually he adapted to the shipboard routine, climbing rigging without fear and responding to commands as the nautical language became more familiar. Then, ready or not, when the call from the masthead came, the young sailor was thrust into the treacherous hunt for the whale.

Six whalemen being tossed out of a boat by the tail of a whale.
Library of Congress

Map Route of Whaling Grounds

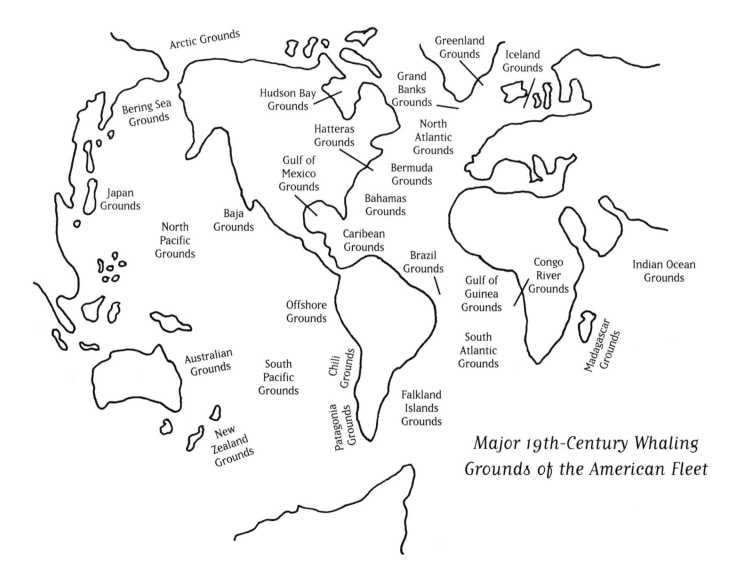

Arctic Grounds

Greenland Grounds

Iceland Grounds

Grand Banks Grounds

Hudson Bay Grounds

Bering Sea Grounds

North Atlantic Grounds

Hatteras Grounds

Japan Grounds

Gulf of Mexico Grounds

Bermuda Grounds

Baja Grounds

Bahamas Grounds

North Pacific Grounds

Caribean Grounds

Brazil Grounds

Congo River Grounds

Indian Ocean Grounds

Gulf of Guinea Grounds

Offshore Grounds

South Atlantic Grounds

Madagascar Grounds

Australian Grounds

South Pacific Grounds

Chili Grounds

New Zealand Grounds

Patagonia Grounds

Falkland Islands Grounds

Major 19th-Century Whaling Grounds of the American Fleet

Whale Tales

Whalemen thought that the whale was a fish because it lived in the ocean and had fins and a tail. It wasn't until the middle of the 19th century that scientists classified the whale as a mammal. Like all mammals, the whale breathes by means of its lungs (through a blowhole), is warm-blooded, and suckles its young instead of hatching eggs as fish do.

Whales are categorized as either toothed or baleen. A toothed whale has two or more teeth and may eat anything from small fish to giant squid. Baleen whales do not have teeth. Instead they have rows of soft, mesh-like cartilage, called *baleen*. Baleen looks like a series of long flexible combs that lie one on top of the other and hang from each side of the whale's jaw. There can be between 100 and 400 pieces on each side! Baleen operates as a strainer, trapping tiny shrimp-like marine animals called krill. Baleen was valuable because it was tough yet flexible. It was used in umbrellas, ladies' corsets, buggy whips, petticoat hoops, and many other products.

Although there are about 80 species of whales, these were the ones most often pursued by whalers:

Right whales They were named right whales because whalers decided they were the right ones to catch. They are easy to catch, float when killed, and produce both baleen and blubber for oil. They average 50 feet (15.24 meters) and 42 tons (38.1 metric tons). The right whale is the one most in danger of extinction (when a species no longer exists) with only a few hundred left in the world. Right whales float when dead because they have a high proportion of fat. Fat is less dense than saltwater, and anything less dense than saltwater will float.

Sperm whales This toothed whale was the one most pursued during the 19th century. The sperm whale's brain is the largest of any creature, weighing 20 pounds (9.07 kilograms)! The *spermaceti*, the waxy substance found in the head, was valuable because it could be used to make smokeless candles and lamps. The sperm whale's teeth were used to make scrimshaw. Males average 50 feet (15.24

meters) in length and weigh between 40 and 60 tons (36.29 and 54.43 metric tons). The sperm whale can dive more than a mile down into the ocean when it searches for giant squid. At those depths there is complete darkness because it is too far down for sunlight to penetrate. Moby Dick, the whale in Herman Melville's book of the same name, was a sperm whale.

Bowhead whales This whale yields the most baleen, as much as 3,000 pounds (1,361 kilograms).

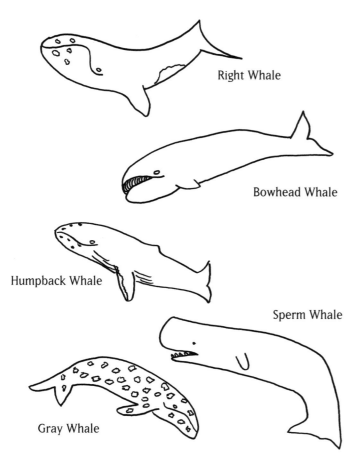

Right Whale

Bowhead Whale

Humpback Whale

Sperm Whale

Gray Whale

Bowheads have a layer of blubber as much as two feet thick. This explains why they are able to tolerate the frigid Arctic waters where they live. They average 60 feet (18.29 meters) and weigh between 60 and 100 tons (54.43 and 90.72 metric tons).

Gray whales These baleen whales, also known as devilfish, are slightly smaller, averaging 45 to 50 feet (13.72 to 15.24 meters) in length and 25 to 40 tons (22.68 to 36.29 metric tons). They were pursued along the Pacific Coast. Whalemen harpooned baby gray whales to trap the mothers. They called them devilfish because they fought like the devil for their young. This whale is a traveler. Each year it migrates from the Arctic Ocean to the Baja Peninsula and back—a distance of about 12,000 miles (19,310 kilometers).

Humpback whales These whales, found in coastal areas, were the least desirable for whalemen because they sink when they're killed. This is because they have a higher ratio of muscle and bone to fat. They average 50 feet (15.24 meters) and weigh about 30 tons (27.22 metric tons). The humpback whale is quite a performer, however, and has entertained sailors for centuries. They *breach*, meaning that they propel their multiton bodies completely above the surface of the ocean, twist around, and then crash back into the water. They also do tricks with their tails, sticking it into the air, turning, and then slapping it down in the water. Humpbacks croon, too. The male humpback can often be heard singing eerie, complicated songs made up of different frequencies.

Nantucket Sleigh Ride: The Chase for the Whale

"There she blows!" the lookout called from the masthead when he spotted a whale. The captain of the whaler peered through his spyglass as the giant whale spouted on the horizon. "Lower away!" he commanded. The whaling crew leaped into action lowering several small whaleboats over the side of the ship for the chase. Each boat raced to be the first to get to the whale.

Five men rowed furiously with their backs to the enormous creature, facing the *boatheader*, who stood at the *stern*, or back, of the boat steering it with a long, heavy oar. He had two jobs: steering the boat and killing the whale with a *lance*, a long, thin metal weapon with an extremely sharp head. The job of boat header was always given to the most experienced officer—sometimes the captain, but more often one of the mates. Alternating between threats and challenges, he pleaded with the oarsmen to go faster: "A dead whale or a *stove* (smashed boat), mates!" "Pull

for your lives!" "I'll give ye rum and tobacco if you catch me that whale!"

When they got within striking distance, the boatheader called, "Give it to him!" and the harpooner or boatsteerer at the *bow*, or front, of the boat quickly put down his oar and picked up his *harpoon*, a 10-foot (3.05-meter) spear. He jumped up, turned, and hurled the harpoon into the creature. Then he hit it with a second harpoon. "Stern all!" the boat header shouted, and the crew backed the boat away from the thrashing whale. Each harpoon had a rope attached at one end. The ropes were hundreds of feet long and were kept coiled up in tubs in the bottom of the small whaleboat. The whalemen let the ropes uncoil as the whale attempted to swim away from them. The purpose of the harpoon was not to kill the whale, but rather to attach the rope to the whale to track it and slow it down. Once a harpoon made its mark, the whale took the crew on a dangerous journey known as a Nantucket sleigh ride. (Nantucket is a port in snowy New England where many early whalemen came from.)

Attached to the whale, the small boat now bounced at lightning speed across the water. The men held tightly to the rope, which grew so hot from the friction that water had to be poured over it. The whale fought mightily to free itself from the harpoon, often staving (smashing) the boat in, capsizing it, or *sounding* (diving deep) so far that the boat went under with it. The injured whale sometimes took the boat so far away that the men would be lost at sea.

Watching Whales

The best way to see whales today is on a whale watch. Many seaports have whale-watch cruises where you can appreciate the magnificent size and beauty of these enormous animals. For a listing of whale-watch cruises all over the world, visit www.whaleguide.com.

Whale fishers; attacking a right whale. *Library of Congress*

But if luck were with them, the whale slowed, and the boatheader called, "Haul in!" The men pulled on the rope and brought the whale closer. Now the boatheader, or lancer, traded places with the harpooner, and he plunged the razor-sharp lance deep into the whale for the final killing thrusts.

The death of the whale was a wrenching sight known as the flurry. The whale swam in frantic circles until its lungs filled with blood instead of air. Great gushes of blood sprayed through its spout-hole, turning the sea crimson. The old sailors proclaimed that the whale had its "chimney afire." Finally, its great body rolled to one side, fin up, and it was dead.

Cutting In and Trying Out

Once the whaling crew successfully slew a 60-ton (54.43-metric-ton) whale, were the men rewarded with a change of dry clothes, something to eat, and a warm bed? Hardly. Their work had just begun. No matter how late the hour or how tired the crew, the whale had to be cut up and boiled before the sharks got to it.

A whaler crew cutting and boiling a whale at sea was a startling sight, often compared to the infernos of hell. Thick clouds of black smoke furled through the ship's masts, and red-hot flames shot into the air. Blood, oil, and blubber sloshed over its decks. Crews on merchant ships often said you could smell a whaler before you saw it. The odor was awful.

The first stage of processing the whale was called *cutting in*. The crew towed the enormous carcass back to the ship, to which it was attached with chains. A narrow platform was hoisted above the whale, where the mates perched while they cut into it with 20-foot (6.10-meter) blades.

If the catch were a sperm whale, the head was cut off and divided into three parts: the *case* (forehead), the *junk* (lower half of the forehead), and the jaw. The case held the valuable oil known as spermaceti. This hardened into a white, waxy substance that the men bailed out in buckets. If the case were too heavy to be lifted into the ship, a man would jump into the head and bail the oil from there. The junk held oil that was less pure, but still valuable, and the jaw yielded teeth. Right, bowhead, and gray whales' jaws were harvested for their baleen.

The fat, or *blubber*, of the whale was stripped from around the whale in a process that was something like peeling an orange. It was cut into one-to-two-ton strips called blanket pieces that were pulled over the side with giant hooks. These slabs were lowered below deck into the blubber room, where they were cut into blocks called horse pieces, and then into smaller pieces that looked like the pages of a book, called bible leaves. The carcass was then tossed back to the sea where ravenous sharks and birds soon devoured it.

The second stage of whale processing was called *trying out*. The bible leaves were fed into enormous pots over a brick stove on deck, called a *tryworks*, where they were boiled for an hour or more and turned into oil. A constant fire, fed first by wood and then by scraps of blubber skimmed from the top of the pots, spewed black, nauseating smoke for miles. A one-foot case filled with seawater, called the goose pen, was placed between the hot fire and the wooden deck to prevent the deck from catching on fire. This stage went on for hours until finally all the blubber had been boiled down. Then the oil was cooled and stored in barrels in the *hold* (space below decks) of the ship. The average whale yielded about 25 to 40 barrels of oil.

During this process the deck and crew were awash in *gurry*—a mix of blood, seawater, and oil. Everything was covered with soot and ash from the trypots. The whalemen's clothes, beds, and even their food reeked of the boiling blubber. The men worked in six-hour watches around the clock until their task was accomplished. Unpleasant as it might seem, this was the business of the whaler, and what everyone worked to achieve. They knew that when the ship's hold was filled with oil, they could go home. The success of voyage was appropriately called greasy luck.

What's That Perfume You're Wearing?

After most of the blubber was stripped, the whalemen would dig for a precious substance called *ambergris*, which was used in the manufacture of perfume. Ambergris was found in the intestines of sick whales. Extremely rare, it was worth hundreds of dollars a pound. Today, because of a nearly worldwide ban on commercial whale hunting (see page 186), the only way to find ambergris is when a whale passes it through its digestive system and it's found floating on the ocean or washed up on the beach.

Make a Whaleboat and Gear

Make a model of the lightweight boat used to slay the mighty whale!

What You Need

For the Boat

A grown-up to assist

Pen

Ruler

12-inch (30.48-centimeter) by 18-inch (45.72-centimeter) by 2-millimeter-thick white foam sheet (available in craft stores)

Scissors

Stapler

Knife

6 craft sticks

For the Whaling Gear

2 ¹⁄₁₆-inch (.158-centimeter) diameter aluminum tubes, 12 inches (30.48 centimeters) long (available in hardware stores)

2 1-inch (2.54-centimeter) by 15-inch (38.1-centimeter) strips from a brown grocery store bag

2 craft sticks

All-purpose glue

1 round wooden dowel ¼ inch (6.35 millimeters) thick and 12 inches (30.48 centimeters) long (available in craft stores)

Layer of newspaper

3 jar or bottle covers—small, medium, and large (You may also use the bottom inch [2.54 centimeters] of a paper or foam cup.)

Tan acrylic paint (poured in paper cup)

Paintbrush

2 yards (1.83 meters) tan colored yarn

Pencil

Beach ball

What You Do

The Boat

1. Draw the boat shape onto the foam according to the diagram. Use your ruler to make the lines.
2. Cut it out.
3. Pinch the two foam edges on one side and curl in toward the middle of the foam. Staple edges together close to the edge. Repeat on the other side.
4. Now fold the boat in half lengthwise.
5. Ask an adult to help you poke six small slits about ¼ inch (6.35 millimeters) down from the top. The knife should cut through both layers, making 12 slits in total. Keep the slits small enough for the craft sticks to fit in snugly.
6. Open the boat and slide the sticks in to look like the seats in a boat. They will stick out a bit on the sides.

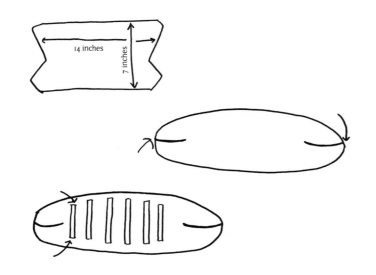

The Whaling Gear

Whaleboats carried about 1,000 pounds (453.6 kilograms) of equipment. We will make a few of the items, including a harpoon, a lance, two oars, a main-line tub with rope, a reserve-line tub with rope, and a bailing bucket.

Harpoon

1. Very gently bend a piece of the aluminum tube into a loop as shown in the diagram.
2. At the other end measure about four inches up from the bottom and gently bend back and forth until the piece breaks off. Discard this piece.
3. Bend 1 inch (2.54 centimeters) of the remaining tube up from the bottom. You will use this to secure the paper that wraps around the bottom of the tube in the next step.
4. Now tuck one end of a strip of paper under this piece and tightly wrap it around and around the tube to make it look like a wooden handle. Stop about halfway up and secure with glue.

Lance

1. Bend one end to make it look like the diagram. The rest of the weapon is made exactly like the harpoon, but because it is longer, you do not need to break off a piece.

69

Oars

1. Have an adult cut the dowel exactly in half.
2. Glue the dowel halfway up a craft stick.
3. Repeat with the remaining dowel and stick.

Tubs and Bailing Bucket

1. Spread a layer of newspaper to cover your work space.
2. Paint the three jar or bottle covers with tan paint. This may take two coats, but it dries quickly.
3. Coil pieces of yarn around the pencil, and then slip off into each of the two larger covers to look like coils of rope in a tub. You may leave loose or secure with glue. The smallest cover will be the bailing bucket.
4. Place the equipment in the whaleboat. Blow up the beach ball and position next to the whaleboat. That's how big the whale was next to the whaleboat! Would you be scared?

Why Whales?

In the early 1600s, when the early settlers arrived in America, they struggled to produce enough crops to feed their families. Because they lived along the coast, they naturally soon looked to the sea as a potentially easier and more reliable food source. The settlers observed as the Native Americans hunted right whales from their canoes. They used harpoons attached to wooden blocks called *drogues* to slow the whale down enough to lance it.

Early Americans learned from the Native Americans, then began to pursue whales in earnest. They progressed from shore whaling to sailing along the coast in search of whales. Colonists on Long Island hunted the right whale on the open sea, stored it onboard, and then brought it to shore to be boiled down into oil. The practice spread, and by the early 1700s the right whale had been hunted nearly to extinction. But a new breed of whale had been discovered off the shore of Nantucket, Massachusetts—the sperm whale.

Sperm whales were faster than right whales, so it became necessary to attach the harpoon to rope. Because sperm whales lived in deeper waters, the hunters had to venture farther and farther out to sea to hunt them. The sperm whale yielded a new source of income for the hunters. People were willing to pay a high price for the clear spermaceti oil, as well as for the rare ambergris. Soon sperm oil burned in all the lamps of the New World. As the typical time for a sperm whaling mission stretched from days to months to years, it became impossible to go ashore to boil down the blubber. Enormous brick tryworks were built onboard ships. Whalers became floating factories where blubber was processed into oil.

In the 1700s, Nantucket became the hub of the sperm whale industry. Sperm whales made ship owners rich and created a society of people to support the industry: sailmakers, hoopers, shipbuilders, riggers, ropemakers, chandlers (proprietors of shops that specialized in goods used aboard ship), and more.

The Revolutionary War (when the American colonies fought Great Britain to become independent, 1775–1783) nearly wiped out Nantucket's whaling industry. British frigates captured American whalers and pressed (forced) them into the navy, into service for the king. Nantucket lost 134 out of 150 whaling ships, but the business sprang back rapidly after the war. In the War of 1812 (when Americans again took up arms against the British for interfering with trade and pressing seamen into service) the British again tried to take American whaling ships into service, but this time the Americans had a bigger and stronger force. The U.S. frigate *Essex* recaptured the American ships and nearly destroyed the entire British whaling fleet.

As sperm whales became scarce in the Atlantic, bigger ships were built and voyages ventured into the Pacific, Arctic, and Indian oceans for up to four years. Nantucket Harbor, which had a shallow entrance, was not safe for the bigger, heavier ships. New Bedford, Massachusetts, with its deepwater harbor, soon replaced Nantucket as the whaling capital of the world. In the mid-1800s more than 735 New Bedford whaling ships, made in New England shipyards, roamed the seas. This was the era known as the golden age of whaling (1820–1850).

The decline of American whaling began when crews deserted to search for gold during the California Gold Rush of 1849 and when Confederate forces sank dozens of whaling ships during the Civil War (1861–1865). When the war was over, the whaling industry rebounded for a while, due to an increased demand for baleen. More ships were lost in the 1870s Arctic disasters, when whalers hunting for bowheads and became trapped in ice. The fatal blow to the whale oil trade occurred with the 1859 discovery of petroleum oil, which quickly replaced whale oil and spermaceti for lighting. Spring steel was invented in 1906; this marked the end of the baleen trade. The whaling industry came to an end. The last ships sailed in the 1920s.

The Last Whaler

The only remaining whaler left in the world is the *Charles W. Morgan*, built in 1841. It ended its last voyage on May 28, 1921, with a cargo of 700 barrels of sperm oil. The ship has been carefully maintained and is the number one attraction at the Mystic Seaport Museum in Mystic, Connecticut.

Fix Plum Duff

Plum duff was the sailor's favorite treat. Only a *hell ship* (one that didn't treat the crew well) didn't serve duff on Sunday. On a good ship it was served twice a week. Treat yourself to this steamed sweet pudding that's almost like a cake. Although the sailors had to settle for molasses sauce, we can eat it with whipped cream!

What You Need

A grown-up to assist
Small to medium metal bowl that fits inside a 5-quart (4.73-liter) lidded slow cooker or crockpot
Sheet of paper towel
Butter or other shortening
2 medium mixing bowls
3 cups (300 grams) flour
1 teaspoon (5 grams) baking soda
1 teaspoon (5 grams) salt
Mixing spoon
1 cup (about 150 grams) chopped suet (beef fat found in meat section of grocery store)
Paring knife
1 cup (237 milliliters) molasses
1 cup (237 milliliters) milk
1 cup (about 170 grams) raisins
Aluminum foil
½ cup (118 milliliters) water
5-quart (4.73-liter) or larger slow cooker (crockpot)
Whipped cream

What You Do

1. Grease the metal bowl with the paper towel and shortening, and set it aside.
2. Mix the flour, baking soda, and salt in one mixing bowl.

3. Chop the suet into fine pieces and mix it with the molasses and milk in the other bowl. Stir thoroughly, making sure the suet does not clump together.

4. Add the dry ingredients to the wet ingredients a little at a time and mix well. By the end it will be thick and difficult to stir.

5. Fold in the raisins.

6. Spoon the mixture into the greased bowl. Cover tightly with aluminum foil.

7. Pour ½ cup of water into the bottom of the slow cooker.

8. Place the bowl in the middle of cooker and cover.

9. Cook on high for 3½ hours.

10. Remove the bowl and release the duff upside down onto a plate. Slice while it is still warm, and top it with whipped cream.

Yield: 10 to 12 servings

The Arctic Fleet: Trapped in Ice

By 1848, American whalemen were seeking new whaling grounds. Over the past half-century they had severely depleted the supply of sperm whales in the Atlantic, Pacific, and Indian oceans. Their pursuit of new waters took them farther and farther from home.

Captain Thomas Roys discovered large numbers of bowhead whales in the Bering Sea, which lies between Alaska and Russia. It connects with the Arctic Ocean through a narrow body of water known as the Bering Strait. It was here and in the Arctic Ocean that whaling was reborn.

The bowhead whale offered even more attractive financial prospects than the sperm whale. A mature bowhead whale might yield 300 barrels of oil com-pared to 45 barrels of oil for a sperm whale. Not surprisingly the news spread and there was a rush to the new whaling grounds.

The weather in the Arctic is harsh and unforgiving. Enormous chunks of ice crash and push, choking and covering the seas; winds reach gale force and whip the seas to turbulence; snow pounds down relentlessly, covering ships and masts with ice. The air is thick with fog and mist. Temperatures dip far below freezing.

In such a climate, a disaster was bound to occur. In 1871, the Inuits, native people of the Arctic, predicted a severe season and warned the 40-vessel whaling fleet to leave before the ice settled in. The Inuits, living close to nature, had observed ice floes in the

spring that had stayed for months instead of the usual days. But the captains ignored the natives' warnings, and in September of 1871, 33 ships became trapped in ice in the Arctic Ocean. Amazingly, the 1,200 officers, crew members, women, and children were saved when they carefully navigated 60 miles (96.56 kilometers) around the ice in their small whaling boats, to whalers that transported them to Honolulu.

This disaster contributed heavily to the decline of the whaling industry. Other Arctic disasters followed. One of the worst was when 12 ships were trapped in 1876 and 50 men died.

Abandonment of the Whalers in the Arctic Ocean, September 1871.
Peabody Essex Museum

Experiment with an Iceberg

One of the most treacherous aspects of whaling in the Arctic Ocean was the constant threat of icebergs. An iceberg is an enormous floating mass of ice that has broken away from a glacier. Only 10 percent of an iceberg is above water, so the danger is that an iceberg can smash a hole in the bottom of the ship when it appears to be far away.

An interesting question about icebergs is: if cold water sinks, why do giant icebergs float?

The answer is that cold water sinks until it reaches the freezing point of 32°F (0°C). When it freezes, it actually becomes lighter. Make your own icebergs and see for yourself.

What You Need

3 or more different bowls
    and cups
Cold tap water
Blue food coloring
Spoon

Freezer
Large clear bowl or con-
    tainer, at least 5 inches
    (12.7 centimeters) deep
Warm tap water

What You Do

1. Fill the bowls and cups with cold water, leaving a little space at the top of each.
2. Add a few drops of blue food coloring to each bowl and mix with a spoon.
3. Carefully place the cups and bowls flat in the freezer. Wait at least 24 hours for the water to freeze.
4. Fill the large bowl with warm water.
5. Loosen the now frozen blue water from the bowls and cups by running warm water over the bottoms.
6. Once they are loosened, drop your icebergs into the large bowl. Now you have floating icebergs! Watch through the side to see the blue water, the cold water, sink as the ice melts.

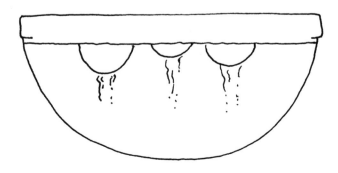

The Wreck of the Whaleship Essex

One of the most terrifying and amazing true stories of the sea is the tragedy of the whaleship *Essex*. On November 20, 1820, the whaling crew had been on an ordinary chase for a whale. One of the whaleboats was struck and damaged by the whale's tail. The men brought the boat back to the main ship for repairs. Suddenly an 85-foot (25.91-meter) whale rammed into the *Essex*. Before they even had time to start the pumps (all wooden ships leaked somewhat, so pumps were always onboard to bail water), the whale came at them again, completely staving in the bow. This was unheard-of, a whale attacking a ship!

The other men in their whaleboats could see the ship leaning to one side and hurried back to see what had happened. They could hardly believe their eyes. The captain, a man named George Pollard, cried out to the first mate, "My God, Mr. Chase, what is the matter?" And the mate answered, "We have been stove by a whale." The men quickly abandoned ship. The ship's steward bravely swam below decks to rescue navigational equipment. They saved all the fresh water and hardtack they could before the ship sank. In the three tiny whaleboats over the next few days, they watched as their mighty ship sank.

Stuck at sea in smallish boats, the whalemen considered their options. Unfortunately they were ignorant of which Pacific islands were friendly and which might have hostile cannibals. Because of their fear, they made a terrible decision. Instead of sailing the 1,500 miles (2.414 kilometers) to Tahiti, which at that time had been visited by Christian missionaries for more than 20 years and was perfectly safe, they decided to travel more than 3,000 miles (4.828 kilometers) to the coast of South America.

One of the whaleboats was stove in again by a whale, but the whalemen were able to fix it by nailing thin strips of wood on the inside of the broken section.

Nearly dead from dehydration, they accidentally discovered an uninhabited island. They thought they had found salvation at last! But the island had little fresh water, and they exhausted its paltry resources of birds and crabs within days. When they found the skeletons of eight men in a cave on the island, they realized that others had been shipwrecked there and died.

Three men took their chances and stayed behind. The rest of the crew made the hard choice to go back in the whaleboats with a new destination—Easter Island—1,200 miles (1,931 kilometers) away. The captain had mistakenly thought they were on Ducie Island. After two months on the open ocean, the first man died of dehydration and was buried at sea. Soon after, a storm separated one of the boats from the other two. When one of the remaining two boats separated from the other, the men on the straying ship were doomed because they had no navigational equipment. Those men were never heard from again.

Now miles away from each other, the two remaining boats fought starvation. A second man died and was buried at sea. When a third man died, the others made the difficult decision to eat the body instead of throwing it overboard. It had been two months since the shipwreck.

When the men in one boat felt themselves close to dying, they made the most horrifying decision of all. They decided to cast lots to sacrifice one person to die so that the others could eat him. A young man, the fourteen-year-old cousin of the captain, drew the short stick. He declared bravely about his lot, "I like it as well as any other." Then the men drew lots again to determine which one would shoot him. This grisly job fell to the young man's best friend.

After 82 days at sea, a British brig picked up Chase's whaleboat. Five days later a Nantucket whaleship rescued Captain Pollard and another survivor, Charles Ramsdell. The rescuers were shocked by the sight of the men, who looked like skeletons and were covered with sores from the salt water, and were surrounded by the bones of their fellow sailors.

Two months later a ship rescued the three men who had stayed behind on the island. They were near death from dehydration and starvation as well.

This is the true-life story that inspired Herman Melville to write the greatest sea novel of all time, *Moby Dick*.

79

The True Tale

For a riveting account read

***Revenge of the Whale: The True Story of the Whaleship Essex*, by Nathaniel Philbrick.**

Carve Scrimshaw

Whalemen had many idle hours at sea to fill. A pleasant way to pass the time was to carve intricate designs into whale teeth and bones to make gifts. Sometimes they applied ink to the designs. This uniquely American folk art is known as *scrimshaw*. Sailors etched pictures of the world around them: sailing ships, whaling scenes, birds, fish, and flowers. They made jewelry, rolling pins, doorstops, cane handles, ship models, pastry crimpers known as jagging wheels, and many other household items.

Most scrimshaw was made from the teeth and bones of the sperm whale or walrus. A favorite gift for sweethearts and wives were corset busks, long strips of baleen that women wore inside their corsets (an undergarment designed to pull the waist in). Many of these creations, depending on the skill of the sailor, were quite elaborate in their design.

Here's a fun way to make scrimshaw with soap!

Scrimshaw tooth with whaling scene. *Peabody Essex Museum*

What You Need

Paper
Pencil
Layer of newspaper
Bar of white soap
Long nail
Cotton swab
Bottle of black ink (available in stationery and craft stores)
Paper towel, moistened

What You Do

1. On a large sheet of paper, use a pencil to practice drawing simple designs—the simpler, the better—of clipper ships, whales, dolphins, flowers, or birds on your paper. (Try www.enchantedlearning.com for some simple line drawings to copy.)

2. Lay down the newspaper to form your work space.

3. Now use the nail like a pencil and etch your design into the soap. A larger nail will give you more control. As you carve, wipe away the excess soap chips. The deeper you make the lines, the better the ink will sink in.

4. Dip a cotton swab into the ink. (This is permanent ink, so be careful not to get it on your clothes.) Spread the inked swab over the entire design.

5. Wipe the surface of the soap with a damp paper towel. This will leave a beautiful black etching over the white soap. Now you're a scrimshander—a person who practices the craft of scrimshaw.

Make a Walking Stick

Walking sticks or canes were used by many fashionable men, women, and even children during the 1800s. Whether young or old, rich or poor, the walking stick was a symbol of dignity. One of the more curious types of walking sticks was the type that was hollowed out for the user to carry or hide things in such as a knife or alcohol!

Although the most common material used to make walking sticks was wood, they were also made of cane, bamboo, ivory, and even glass! Naturally, the whaleman made his walking sticks out of whalebone and whale teeth. The handles on whaling canes were carved into shapes such as snakes, women's legs, bald eagles, and Turks' head knots, many lavishly decorated with scrimshaw. Several of these canes have survived and can be seen in seaport museums.

What You Need

30-inch (76.2-centimeter) length of white PVC pipe (Note: PVC pipe is sold inexpensively in hardware stores, usually in 5-foot [1.52-meter] lengths. Ask the store to cut it for you.)

1-inch (2.54 centimeter) piece of white PVC pipe

Precut PVC connection pieces:

1 ½-inch (1.27 centimeters) white tee

1 ½-inch (1.27 centimeters) white 45° elbow

2 ½-inch (1.27 centimeters) white plug spigots

White acrylic paint (optional)

Paintbrush (optional)

Fine-point permanent black marker pen (optional)

What You Do

1. Once the pipe is cut, you can assemble the pieces in less than a minute with no glue. First attach the tee to the top of the 30-inch (76.2-centimeter) piece of pipe.
2. Attach the 1-inch (2.54-centimeter) piece of pipe to one side of the tee.
3. Attach the 45° elbow to that piece.
4. Put one of the plugs at the end of the elbow.
5. Attach the other plug to the other side of the tee piece. Now you have a walking stick! If you want to decorate the top of the cane, paint it and draw fancy scrimshaw-type designs with the marker.

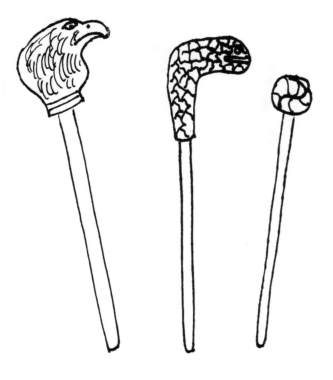

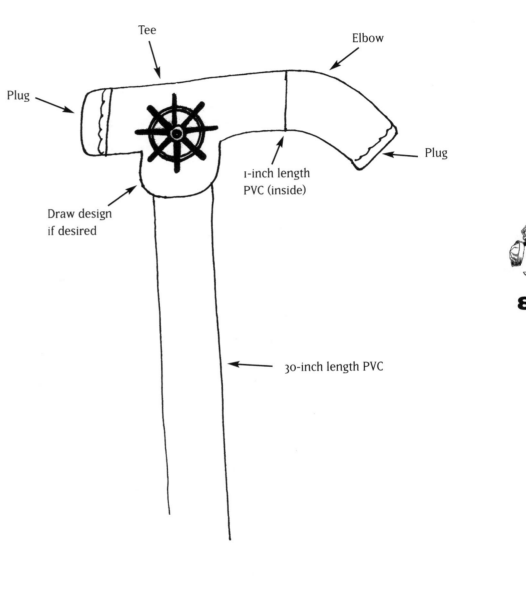

Tee

Elbow

Plug

Plug

1-inch length PVC (inside)

Draw design if desired

30-inch length PVC

Keep a Logbook and Make a Whale Stamp

The logbook was the official record of the whaling voyage. Keeping the logbook was the first mate's responsibility. Each entry was dated and included the latitude and longitude of the ship's location, the weather, the names of the ships communicated with, gams, injuries, deaths, ports of call, and sometimes sea animals the crew caught, such as turtles, porpoises, and fish. The most important notations in the logbook were always the number of whales sighted, chased, and slaughtered—and the barrels of oil rendered. Log keepers used these drawings and stamps to illustrate the story of the whaling voyage.

Full whale, head up: A whale was successfully captured.

Full whale, head down: A whale was killed but sank before it was retrieved.

Half whale, flukes up: A whale was sighted and then got away.

Half whale, head up: A whale was harpooned and then escaped.

Whale stamps were usually carved in wood or whalebone, and a ship would carry them in a set. Here's how you can make your own.

What You Need

4 ounces (113.4 grams) lightweight air-dry modeling compound
Pen or large paper clip, untwisted
Layer of newspaper
Dark water-based marker or black India ink and paintbrush
Paper

What You Do

1. To make all four stamps, divide the compound into four sections. With each mound, pull off a small piece to use as a handle and set aside.
2. Flatten the modeling material to an oval about ½ inch (1.27 centimeters) thick, measuring approximately 2½ inches (6.35 centimeters) by 5 inches (12.7 centimeters).
3. Draw the whale design lightly in pen or just carve it directly into the material with the paper clip, making the grooves quite deep. If you make a mistake, just roll the compound and start over again.

4. Roll the pieces you set aside for handles into thick logs and press them onto the stamp backs.
5. Let dry for 24 hours. The stamps will be soft and flexible when dry.
6. Lay down a layer of newspaper.
7. Color a whale with the marker (or paint over it with India ink). To get a really good impression, go over it twice.
8. Quickly press the inked stamp onto a piece of paper, pushing the stamp down evenly with your fingers. Lift.

In our next chapter we'll explore the world of merchant sailors—men who sailed the world in ships full of the raw goods of the young country. In exchange they brought home the sights and treasures of the Old World. Much of Chapter 3 is focused on China, because the bulk of what was imported—tea, silk, and porcelain—was from there.

3
The Sea Traders

Anchors aweigh! Come aboard for our merchant-ship journey. We'll sail on mighty clipper ships, packet ships that always run on time, ruthless pirate ships, brutal slave ships, blockade-running ships, and ships that trade American goods. We'll meet the crews and learn about their duties and the colorful places they sail in search of cargo. We'll make a Chinese plate and a ship's bell, then watch as the spectacular clipper ships slice through the seas at greater and greater speeds. You'll be amazed at the story of the mutiny on the slave ship *Amistad.* You'll make a lighthouse like the ones that guided the sailing ships. We'll take a crack at sending Morse code, hear a real pirate story, and learn to tie knots like an old salt.

Yankee maritime merchants were in every way like their new country—young, bold, and confident. Traders in foreign ports were surprised to do business with a captain who was only 19 or 20 years old. These young merchants reflected the American mood after the country's victory in the Revolutionary War against Great Britain. Americans were open and eager for new opportunities and willing to travel to the far reaches of the Earth for them.

In the years following the Revolution, great tall-masted ships sailed the seven seas to trade the raw materials America had to offer: cotton, hemp, tobacco, wheat, flax, whale oil, ship timber, tar, beef and pork products, lumber, beeswax, hides from California, and even ice from New England ponds and lakes. American manufactured products soon followed: textiles, spermaceti candles, rum, brandy, chocolate, soap, pottery, barrels, and leather goods.

Slavery was also part of our merchant marine past, part of the triangular trade route. In one route, Newport ships brought molasses and sugar from the West Indies to be made into rum in America. The rum was then sold to African slavers in exchange for slaves. The slaves were transported across the ocean and sold in the Americas and the West Indies. Molasses and sugar were brought back to North and South America for the cycle to continue.

Pirates Supported by Our Government

Merchant ships played an interesting role during wartime as *privateers*. During the Revolutionary War, George Washington allowed merchant vessels to capture British supply ships. This was the equivalent of getting permission from the government to act like a pirate and take over enemy ships during wartime. Again, when the War of 1812 broke out, the Americans depended on private ships because the

Clipper ship *Great Republic*. Check out its size: length of deck, 325 feet (99.06 meters); breadth of beam, 53 feet (16.15 meters); depth of hold, 39 feet (11.89 meters); tonnage per register, 4,500. (Remember that one ton equals 2,000 pounds [907.2 kilograms]!) *Library of Congress*

United States Navy was so small. Privateers were issued letters of marque from the United States government giving them permission to capture enemy British ships as prizes. The Confederacy used privateers during the Civil War because they had so few ships to fight the U.S. Navy.

Armed with guns, the privateers would board a captured vessel and sail it back to their home port. There they sold the ship and goods at auction and split the proceeds between the privateer's crew and owner.

Merchants in the Revolutionary War, the War of 1812, and the Civil War all engaged in *blockade running*. When a country is at war, a blockade prevents ships from leaving to trade with other countries. American merchant ships ran through British blockades in the Revolutionary War and the War of 1812. During the Civil War, the Union had a crippling blockade against the South. Confederate merchant ships had limited success in getting through it, even with the help of Great Britain.

Reliable Sea Travel for People and Goods

The first reliable form of sea travel for passengers began in the mid-1800s with the packet ships. With regular schedules and affordable prices, thousands of people *emigrated* (left their country of origin to live elsewhere) across the seas to "the land of opportunity."

Ships returning home from the East and West were floating warehouses of international treasure: Chinese porcelain, tea, and silk; spices from Sumatra; salt from Spain; wine from Portugal, Spain, and France; English woolens and Irish linens; manufactured iron and steel products from different parts of Europe; Arabian coffee; cloth from India; African ivory and gold; fruit from South America and the West Indies; lemons and olive oil from the Mediterranean; iron from Russia and Sweden; and figs from Turkey. There were few regions of the world during the age of sail where Americans did not find something to trade for.

Map of the Trading Routes

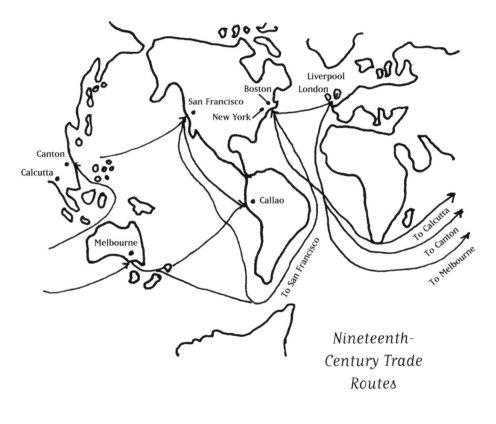

Nineteenth-Century Trade Routes

Full Speed Ahead: Life Aboard a Merchant Ship

New England seagoing families often encouraged their young sons of 13 or 14 to become a cabin boy aboard a merchant ship. It was a well-respected way to teach the son the family business by signing him on with a family member or friend. These boys learned the basics of sailing, assisted the sailors, and absorbed the language and the rituals of seaboard life. On a good ship they learned how to steer at the helm and use navigational instruments. Many went on to become officers and captains themselves.

As the age of sail progressed, events enticed the young recruits elsewhere. Gold was discovered in California in 1848, factory jobs opened up in the east, and middle to western America needed a new force of farmhands. The common seaman's pay was low and the work could be grinding and dangerous. Young men with promise began to turn away from the sea. In the second half of the 19th century many ships had their share of scoundrels, criminals, drunks, and uneducated hands to fill out the crews. This new breed of sailors was called packet rats after the packet ships, which delivered mail, passengers, and cargo. (Read more about this on page 129.)

The Crew

The crew aboard a merchant ship included the officers, the idlers, and the seamen. The officers included the captain and his first and second mate. Many merchant ships also carried a *supercargo*, an officer in charge of selling and trading the ship's cargo. Next in rank came the idlers: the cook; the carpenter; the *boatswain*, the man who was in charge of the ship's maintenance; and one or more stewards. The bulk of the crew were the able-bodied seamen, sailors who could steer a ship, work the rigging, and perform all the ordinary sailor's duties with skill; the ordinary seamen, who could tie standard knots, set and furl sails, and had a basic understanding of the rigging; and the cabin boys.

Keeping Track of Time

Time at sea was measured not in hours, but in bells. When the ship's clock struck on the hour and the half hour, the helmsman rang the ship's bell behind him. Upon hearing it, the crew member closest to the bell in the fo'c'sle then rang that bell the same number of times. This prompted the man on lookout to call out, "Six bells and all is well!" (or however many bells had rung).

The bells corresponded to a four-hour watch, which was how long each man was on duty. The first bell was rung after the first half hour of the watch was over, two bells were rung when the first hour was over, and so on until the end of the watch.

Let's say the watch was from midnight to four o'clock in the morning. The bells were rung like this:

12:30 A.M.: one bell
1:00 A.M.: two bells
1:30 A.M.: three bells
2:00 A.M.: four bells
2:30 A.M.: five bells

3:00 A.M.: six bells
3:30 A.M.: seven bells
4:00 A.M.: eight bells

Duties on Watch

As soon as the voyage got underway, the men were divided into two groups, the *larboard watch* and the *starboard watch*. Larboard watch was renamed *port watch* in later years to avoid confusion because the words *larboard* and *starboard* sound so similar. The first and second mates would choose whom they wanted to work for them during the journey. In keeping with maritime tradition, the first mate's crew, the larboard watch, was responsible for the left and forward parts of the ship. The starboard watch was the second mate's crew. Their duties were to take care of the right and *aft* (back) parts of the ship. Each mate carefully chose the men he thought to be most seaworthy. Watches swapped deck duty for sleeping time, all day and night, four hours on deck, four hours to sleep (and never more!). The only exception was from 4:00 P.M. to 8:00 P.M. when the watch was broken up into two watches called the first and second dogwatches. These were from 4:00 to 6:00 and 6:00 to 8:00, so sailors wouldn't be on duty the same hours every day.

What did they do on watch? They labored at a never-ending series of chores and duties. Officers were afraid of idle time, thinking it would lead to trouble on a ship with men cooped up for months at a time. Merchant sailors didn't have the dangerous dirty work that the whalemen did, but operating a square-rigger on the open ocean was a colossal task all on its own.

Here is a list of the chores necessary for a well-run ship.

Hoist that bail! Swab that deck! Buckets of seawater were pulled over the side for the mate to throw on the deck. The men then scrubbed the wooden planks clean with brooms.

Sand the deck This chore was known as holystoning. The decks were sprinkled with sand and then scrubbed with a large, soft stone. Smaller stones called prayer books were used to get into the small cracks. When they were finished, the sailors prayed for rain so that they didn't have to hoist up all the seawater it took to swab it off!

Polish the bell All the brass trim and fixtures had to glisten aboard ship. It was a sign of pride, signifying that the captain kept his ship in top condition.

Sand and polish the wood The wood trim, constantly battered by the ocean air and water, had to be regularly sanded and varnished. This was a tedious job usually given to greenhands.

Tar the rigging Every few months the ship's rigging had to be waterproofed by spreading tar on every inch from the masthead down. The work was dirty, and it was dangerous because there weren't any safety nets to catch a sailor if he fell.

Slop on slush This task was similar to tarring. The masts were regularly rubbed down with fat boiled out of the men's salted beef. This was messy, slippery, and dangerous work.

Collect oakum Old ropes were pulled apart and mixed with tar to make oakum. This was used to caulk seams between wood planks. Sailors didn't seem to mind this simple, mundane task.

Here is a list of essential sailor's duties.

Man the helm Day and night a man had to be at the helm to keep the ship on course. In stormy weather, it took two men to steer as the ship pitched under them and waves crashed over their heads onto the decks. Men on deck during a storm were always in danger of being swept overboard.

Stand lookout The lookout stood at the bow to watch for storms, land, icebergs, and other ships.

Trim the sails Sails had to be set, furled, and trimmed according to the angle of the wind. There was a complex system of ropes, masts, and sails, each with its own purpose.

Brace the yards After the sails had been set, the yards had to be pivoted (turned) to take advantage of the wind.

Hoist the cargo Once the ship was in port, the business of unloading cargo commenced. This was a pleasant time for the sailors, who knew that liberty soon followed.

Anchors aweigh! A ship's anchor weighed several hundred pounds (kilograms) and even with the help of the *capstan* (a mechanical winch) it took hours to hoist.

Food and Entertainment Aboard Ship

Meals for the crew were bland and unappetizing. Breakfast was a porridge of cornmeal mush and molasses. The rest of the meals were usually some combination of salted meat and hardtack.

The dogwatch was when sailors could relax. They sang sea chanteys, played music, and danced. They sat on their sea chests and smoked their pipes. Often a few sailors would spin their yarns. Others might teach a greenhand how to tie a Turk's head (a prized, difficult knot) or carve a model ship. But even the most hardened sailor's conversation eventually returned to memories of home and the people he'd left behind.

Make a Sewing Palm

Sailors were skilled at using needle and thread. They had to repair sails that were battered and ripped at sea, as well as tend to their own mending of worn and ripped clothing. Their needlework eventually extended to free time as well. To pass the time, many sailors made quilts, rugs, and other decorative textiles.

The sewing palm was an important item in the sailor's ditty box, which held his sailmaking supplies. It was useful for sewing heavy materials such as canvas with a large needle. The sewing palm was a strip of leather that stretched over the palm and thumb and was tied on the back of the hand. In the middle of the palm was a piece of metal with indentations that allowed the sailmaker to press the butt of the needle in as he sewed. It protected his hand in much the same way a thimble protects a finger. You can make your own sewing palm with this activity.

What You Need

1 strip of vinyl or leather 12 inches (30.48 centimeters) by 2½ inches (6.35 centimeters) (available in small pieces at fabric stores)

Quarter

Pen

Scissors

Solid metal button larger than a quarter with a bumpy (not smooth) surface and the hole for attaching the thread underneath

Heavy-duty thread

Heavy sewing needle

Hole punch

Shoelace

What You Do

1. In the middle of the vinyl strip, outline the quarter in pen.
2. Cut out the round hole with the scissors. Slip the hole over the thumb of the hand you use to write.
3. Put a mark on the vinyl, just a little bit closer to your thumb than the middle of your palm. This is where the button will go.
4. Take off the strip and sew the button on this mark so that it is next to the hole.
5. Put the strip back over your thumb and around the back of your hand. Cut the strip in the back so that each side just meets.
6. Take off the strip and punch a hole at the end of each side.
7. Pull the shoelace through the holes.
8. Put the strip back over your hand and tie it or ask someone for help to tie it.
9. Use the button to press the butt or end of the needle through some thick material.

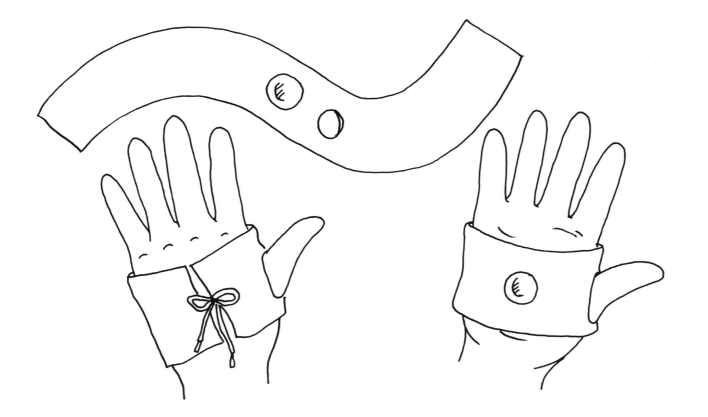

Construct a Ship's Bell

The ship's brass bell marked the long hours at sea. It was rung every half hour. The bell was also used to signal the ship's presence in foggy conditions or as an alarm in an emergency.

What You Need

Layer of newspaper
Paintbrush
Gold acrylic paint
4-inch diameter (10.16-centimeter) clay flowerpot with at least one hole in the bottom
Wooden bead larger than the opening in the bottom of the flowerpot (available in craft stores)

Red paint pen
18-inch (45.72-centimeter) strand of gold wire, ribbon, or string
1 gold jingle bell up to one inch (2.54 centimeters) wide (Available in craft stores. The larger the bell, the louder the ring.)

What You Do

1. After you lay the newspaper down on the floor or a tabletop, paint the inside and outside of the pot and the wood bead gold. Use two coats if necessary and let dry.
2. Tip the pot upside down. Decide on a ship's name and write it in block letters with the red paint pen.
3. Pull the gold string through the hole in the jingle bell. Even up the ends of the strings. Tie a knot about 3½ inches (8.89 centimeters) from the bell.
4. Now pull the two ends of string through the large bead, then through the top of the pot. Tie again. The bell should now swing freely inside the pot when you hold the ends of the string.
5. Use the bell to wake up a member of your crew tomorrow morning!

Cook Lobscouse

Lobscouse was a favorite meal of the sailors. The cabin scouse was salt beef, potatoes, carrots, and other vegetables cooked together with pounded hardtack. The fo'c'sle scouse was usually only meat, potatoes, and hardtack.

What You Need

A grown-up to assist
Large bowl filled halfway with cold water
1 pound of salt meat (.45 kilograms) (This is more commonly found in Canada. Corned beef may be substituted.)
Colander
Knife
Large pot
Spoon for stirring
4 potatoes
2 large carrots
Vegetable peeler
½ cake of hardtack,* crumbled (Oyster crackers may be substituted.)
Pepper

*Note: Hardtack is available in Newfoundland, Nova Scotia, and other parts of Canada. In the United States you can purchase it from Bent's Cookie Factory in Massachusetts (www.bentscookiefactory.com). Nabisco makes the same cracker under the name Crown Pilot Crackers (sold in the Northeast). Mechanical Baking Company in Illinois also sells hardtack (www.mechanical-bakery.com).

What You Do

1. Soak the meat in a bowl of cold water overnight to remove some of the salt.
2. Drain in the colander.
3. With an adult's help, cut the meat into cubes and put in the pot with enough cold water to cover.
4. Cook for one hour over medium heat, stirring occasionally.
5. With the help of an adult, peel and cut the potatoes and carrots into cubes and add to the beef.
6. Cook for 15 minutes or until the vegetables are cooked through.
7. Add the hardtack and pepper and simmer for 5 minutes.

Yield: 4 to 6 servings

Pirate Attack!

On September 20, 1832, a merchant ship from Salem, Massachusetts, was bound for Rio de Janeiro. Her cargo was $20,000 in silver, 100 bags of saltpeter (a rock salt used in gunpowder, meat curing, and medicines), and 100 chests of tea. The ship was called the *Mexican*. Its captain was John G. Butman. There had been several acts of piracy in recent months against Salem ships, and the captain and crew were especially wary because of the silver they were carrying.

On the 4:00 A.M. watch one morning, the first mate warned the crew that he had seen a vessel in the night, crossing back and forth behind them. The captain looked at the schooner through his spyglass and was able to count 30 men on deck—a very bad sign. The *Mexican* tried to prepare a defense and realized in horror that their cannons were useless because the shot they had was too large to fit into the guns.

The ship pressed in on them at full sail and fired a musket shot. The musket was a gun that was fired from the shoulder. There was no doubt now that a pirate ship was attacking them. The pirate ship was called the *Panda*, and the captain was Don Pedro Gilbert of Spain. His mate was Don Bernardo de Soto, the owner of the ship. The pirates took over the *Mexican*, with orders from their captain to kill everyone onboard. The pirate captain reportedly said, "Dead cats don't mew. Have her thoroughly searched, and bring aboard all you can—you know what to do with them."

The pirates beat the men with swords and clubs, and forced them to bring up the chests of silver to be put aboard the pirate ship. Finally, they locked the sailors below decks and proceeded to destroy everything. They slashed the sails, the rigging, the masts, and yards; then they filled the ship's galley with tar and oakum. Because they seemed to lack the nerve to kill them as the captain had ordered, they decided to burn them alive instead.

They set fire to the galley, and as the ship burst into flames, the men of the pirate ship watched and then sailed away. Captain Butman was able to pull himself through the unlocked skylight and he and his men doused the flames with buckets of water. They crouched on deck and left enough of the fire smoldering to make the pirates think that the ship would burn into the sea. Incredibly, despite the damage to all the sails and rigging, everything was repaired and new sails were flying before nightfall.

On October 12, 1832, the *Mexican* sailed back to Crowninshield's Wharf in Salem harbor, where they told their story to an amazed public. Newspapers all over the country ran the story of the pirate attack. The pirates were captured and brought back to Boston, where they were executed by hanging. Only one pirate escaped the hangman's noose—Don Bernardo de Soto. He was not sentenced to hang because of something he had done in 1831 while the captain of his own ship. De Soto had discovered the Salem ship *Minerva* wrecked on the rocks of one of the islands of the Bahamas. De Soto transported 72 people to the safety of Havana, Cuba, and was awarded a silver cup from the people of Salem for his kindness and bravery. The court of Boston repaid him for this good deed by sparing his life. De Soto turned away from the pirate life and sailed to the West Indies.

Years later an old Salem sea captain recognized the captain of a passenger steamer that ran between Havana and Matanzas, Cuba. It was none other than the former pirate, Don Bernardo de Soto.

Pirate Chest

Here's a treasure trove of pirate facts.

Cruelest pirate Blackbeard (Edward Teach) had a chest-long black beard and stuck lit pieces of rope under his hat to smolder to give him an even more frightening appearance. He cut the fingers off any of his victims who did not hand over their rings. He once made a man eat his own ear.

Women pirates Anne Bonny and Mary Read disguised themselves as men and both ended up on the same pirate ship, headed by Bonny's boyfriend, "Calico Jack" Rackham. In 1720, the pirates were brought to justice. The male crew was hanged, but the women were spared because they were both pregnant.

Modern pirates Pirates are still a threat at sea. About 300 attacks of piracy a year are reported, many of which result in the death of crew members. The worst-hit areas are around the island nations of Southeast Asia.

The Jolly Roger This was the black-and-white flag that a pirate ship used to warn a merchant ship not to resist. They hoped that the frightening symbol of a skull and crossbones would reduce the need for hand-to-hand combat. Each pirate had his own design.

Pirate Island In the early 1700s, the harbor of New Providence in the Bahamas served as a kind of vacation spot for pirates. They spent their time there lying in the sun, eating, drinking, chasing women, fighting, and gambling before they went back to work plundering ships.

Walking the plank There are no well-documented cases of pirates making people do this. More commonly they resorted to outright murder or to marooning, leaving sailors on deserted islands to die.

The real Robinson Crusoe Alexander Selkirk was a Scottish sailor who ran away to become part of a pirate crew. Unable to get along with his pirate captain, he was put ashore on the uninhabited island of Juan Fernandez in 1704. He was not rescued until four years later. His incredible story of survival is the basis of Daniel Defoe's novel *Robinson Crusoe*.

Create Seaweed Pictures

In the 1860s and 1870s hundreds of merchant ships gathered to collect a strange cargo—bird droppings from off the coast of Peru. These bird droppings had accumulated so thickly that they'd become a valuable fertilizer. Known as *guano*, it was dug up by laborers on the Chinchas islets off the coast of Peru and sold to merchants. The islands where the guano was collected were uninhabited.

A little girl named Joanna Colcord remembered when one of the captains' wives noticed that the colorful seaweed of the region made lovely designs when it was allowed to dry onto paper. There is a natural substance in the plant that allows the seaweed to adhere to the paper. This led to a new craze among seagoing women and children that lasted for many years.

This was during the Victorian age (the late 1800s, when Queen Victoria was Queen of England), when art was very ornate and flowery. Typical designs at the time would have included a lot of hearts and flowers. Seascapes were also popular, with real sand, seaweed, and shells.

What You Need

Layer of newspaper
Seaweed collected from the ocean and placed into a
  plastic bag or pail
Bowl of fresh water
Brown grocery bag
Glue (if needed)
Scissors (if needed)
Sand, shells, other natural materials (optional)

What You Do

1. Lay the newspaper out on the floor or table top.
2. Place the seaweed in a bowl of fresh water.
3. Pull the seaweed out of the water and lay it out on the newspapers to get rid of the excess water.
4. Take a small amount of seaweed at a time and press it down on the paper bag.
5. Arrange it into designs of flowers or trees, or make it part of a seascape with other items such as sand and shells (use glue for these). Cut it into small pieces if it is too heavy.
6. Let it dry overnight. If any pieces do not stick after drying, you can use glue to make them adhere to the paper.

Family Life at Sea

Joanna Colcord and her brother Lincoln were both born at sea aboard their father's ship, the *Charlotte A. Littlefield.* Family letters and writings left by the Colcord family tell us a lot about family life at sea in the late 1800s. Joanna went on to write two books about sea chanteys and a book about seafaring language. An interesting book about Joanna and Lincoln Colcord is *Letters from the Sea, 1882–1901: Joanna and Lincoln Colcord's Seafaring Childhood,* by Parker Bishop Albee. This book is for adults, but a good young reader might be able to tackle it.

The China Trade

After the Revolutionary War, the United States was a free but poor nation. There was little money to invest in industry and there were few jobs for soldiers returning from war. In addition, commerce with all European nations was closed to the United States out of fear that similar uprisings would spread to other colonies. Even ports in the West Indies, a place the United States had traded with for years, were closed to U.S. trade. Americans began to look to the Far East for new opportunities.

China! For more than 150 years, direct trade to China had been forbidden to Americans. All trade had to be transacted through the monopoly of the British-owned East India Company. In August 1784 the *Empress of China*, the first American ship to trade with China, entered the Whampoa anchorage, a Portuguese port 12 miles (20.92 kilometers) south of Canton. With typical American swagger, it fired a 13-gun salute to the rest of the Western fleet anchored there. In effect this was the beginning of the America–China trade. The cargo aboard the *Empress* included *ginseng* (an herb the Chinese believed could restore youth), rum, and furs. Trade with China was an experiment, one that the Americans could not resist making now that they were independent of England.

The Chinese had little respect for outside merchants and enforced strict rules governing trade. A typical foreign crew was forced to stay at the Portuguese outpost of Whampoa and wait for their goods to be unloaded and sent to the *hongs*, or warehouses, in Canton. If a captain brought his family, they were also left in Whampoa. The Chinese did not allow Western women to enter Canton.

Canton was the only Chinese port open to foreigners. They could only do business with a group of about 10 to 13 Chinese merchants known as the hong merchants. Because Westerners were not allowed to learn the Chinese language and most Chinese were not inclined to learn English, a new form of communication known as *pidgin English* evolved for the purpose of doing business.

What a colorful sight it must have been for those first Americans as they entered Canton. They saw Chinese junk boats with eyes painted on the bows, joss sticks of powdered sandalwood tossed as offerings to the sea, flower boats, aristocratic Mandarins with two banks of oars, houseboats full of families. They smelled spicy scents of Asian cooking in the air; heard music playing, gongs sounding, and firecrackers exploding; and saw huge warehouses displaying the flags of the world. It was an intoxicating mix for the young sailor half a world away from home.

And what cargo did the Americans bring home to their own country?

China in the early part of the 19th century held the secrets to three internationally desired products. They alone had mastered the art of making silk from the silkworm, manufacturing porcelain china from clay, and cultivating tea from the tea plant. Upon returning to the United States, the *Empress of China* made a large profit on her cargo of these items.

China referred to itself as the Celestial Kingdom, the center of the world. The Chinese believed there was nothing the Americans could offer that they didn't already have. This forced the Americans to search desperately for acceptable cargo. The first shipments of ginseng were well received, but that trade was limited. The Americans next turned to otter furs from the Northwest, trading metals to Native Americans in exchange for the pelts. Eventually the wholesale slaugh-

ter of the otters erased the supply. The bloody seal trade followed. Seals were hunted off the east and west coasts of South America. They were trapped as they came ashore, clubbed with a bat, and then killed with a knife before being skinned. Seals were hunted as the sea otters were until they were near extinction.

Americans constantly were frustrated by their inability to find a trading cargo that equaled tea, porcelain, and silk. They continued to search for unusual and exotic items that the Chinese would buy. They discovered sandalwood, which the Chinese wanted for building temples, burning incense, and making ornamental boxes and chests. This was soon stripped from the hills of the Hawaiian Islands where it grew. Unusual things, too, were sought for food, including the sea slug, or sea cucumber, found on the coral islands in the Pacific, and bird's nests, which were found on the cliffs of Java and Borneo and were boiled to make bird's-nest soup.

There was one product that was always in demand in China, and that was the habit-forming drug opium. Although the Chinese government had outlawed the import of opium in 1800, the drug enjoyed a thriving illegal trade, especially by the British, who made it from poppies grown in their colony of India and were selling it to the Chinese at a huge profit. Americans, weary of the inequitable trade balance between their country and China, saw the opium trade as an equalizer. Although many U.S.

The hongs of Canton, China, 1805. *Peabody Essex Museum*

traders took a moral stand against it, at least 20 percent of America's cargo to China was opium from Turkey, until the Opium War of 1839 put an end to such trade. The Chinese had tried to peacefully end the opium trade for years, but the British refused to cooperate. When the Chinese destroyed thousands of chests of British opium, the British declared war on China. Forced to confront the strength of the ominous British military, the Chinese surrendered and were made to sign treaties that would change East–West trade forever.

Four new ports in China were then opened to foreign trade: Shanghai, located in eastern China where the Yangtze River meets the sea, soon replaced Canton as the center for international trade. Foochow, a seaport on the Min River in southeastern China, became a major tea exporter, along with Amoy in southern China at the mouth of the Jiulong River. Ningbo was located on the Yong River in Eastern China. Hong Kong itself was turned over and became a British colony.

Women from other parts of the world were now allowed to join their husbands in China, and many international settlements sprang up. These settlements had their own laws and places of business. Further pressure on the Chinese allowed for trade on the country's rivers. The Yangtze River ran through provinces rich with agricultural products, coal, manufactured textiles, and tea. The Americans soon had their own ships on these rivers.

But by the mid-1800s America had started to produce and manufacture its own goods, and the desire for Chinese products was on the wane. Americans were making their own fabrics on machine-powered looms. Potteries in New England and Europe were making porcelain. Americans increasingly went to China to *sell* as well as to *buy*.

The days of the old China trade were over by the end of the Civil War, but the prosperity it created was invested in new United States ventures: railroads, banking, industry, and philanthropy all benefited from fortunes made in the China trade.

The Luxury of Silk

Silk! The mere word conjures up images of luxury and wealth. This soft, luxurious fabric was the opposite of the hard-working, pragmatic Yankee's clothing, which was typically made from stiff cotton and wools. As a coveted Chinese import, silk was second only to tea during the old China trade. For 3,000 years the Chinese alone held the secret to the cultivation of silk from the silkworm. It was a secret so highly guarded that anyone who told a foreigner was put to death.

Sericulture, the process of raising silkworms to produce raw silk, was a delicate craft performed only by women. After hatching from eggs, the silkworm caterpillars were placed into bamboo baskets where they were carefully fed washed and chopped mulberry leaves. These leaves grew on trees that were cultivated especially for the silkworms. The worms fed and molted (shed their skins) for 35 days. It took approximately a ton (907.2 kilograms) of leaves to raise an ounce of silkworms! (An ounce [28.35 grams] of worms yields about 12 pounds [5.44 kilograms] of raw silk.)

The next stage was when the worms spun their cocoons. They were transferred to straw bundles called silkworm hills, about 60 or 70 worms to each hill. It takes five days for a silkworm to spin its cocoon. The silk is spun in a continuous figure-eight pattern and is several hundred yards (meters) long. When the spinning was done, the cocoons were placed in very hot water. They were stirred with a bamboo comb until the silk unreeled from the cocoon where it was attached. Now the silk was taken to a reeling (winding) machine. As the machine rotated, the filaments (fibers) were compressed into silk thread. The final step was when the thread was woven into cloth on a machine called a loom.

Merchant sailors filled the holds of their ships with silk of every color. They also brought back silk clothing and paintings on silk as special gifts for their loved ones.

Make a Chinese Plate

othing was more prized to the New England housewife than a set of Chinese porcelain dishes. Even in families that had servants, the china was usually handwashed by the mistress of the house to ensure that it was not broken or chipped. The hostess who served her guests tea from a china tea set was the envy of her neighborhood.

China held the secret to making porcelain 1,000 years before the rest of the world. It was superior because of three essential qualities: hardness, resonance (a ringing sound when tapped), and translucence (the ability for light to pass through). The Chinese made their porcelain from two key ingredients: kaolin, a natural white clay that comes from the earth, and petuntse, which was derived from stone in the mountains along the Ch'ang River. To use the petuntse, they had to go through a lengthy process of washing, pulverizing, and soaking it until the purest part, called the cream, rose to the top. The cream was collected and put through a sieve. Finally it was put into bags of cloth to thicken.

The mixture of these two ingredients gave the porcelain its superior quality. The kaolin made it easy to mold, and the petuntse worked in the heating process to make the porcelain strong.

The kaolin, petuntse, oil, and water were mixed together. Then the mixture went to the potter, who shaped it on his revolving wheel. Each potter made a particular piece of pottery; one might make cups, another plates or bowls. The most skilled craftsmen were the artists who painted the patterns and glazes, most often blue and white or rose and white. The vibrant blue glaze got its color from cobalt oxide. The final glaze was a mixture of petuntse and water.

Next, the porcelain was fired, or baked, in a kiln (oven) made of clay bricks. This took several days with temperatures in the kiln reaching 3,000°F (1,649°C)! The finished porcelain was then placed in huge barrels and transported by waterways all over China, then across the Pacific to the rest of the world.

Americans could purchase *stock* (already made) Chinese porcelain painted with lovely scenes from Chinese life, birds, butterflies, flowers, and other designs, or they could buy unpainted porcelain and a Chinese craftsman would decorate it according to their specifications. A drawing would be sent to Canton, where the Chinese artist would paint to order such things as American eagles, clipper ships, and family crests. Because the artist could not read or understand English, this sometimes led to funny results, such as the plates that read, "Put this picture in the center!"

Today Chinese porcelain from the old China trade is prized by collectors and displayed in museum collections. It is a cherished reminder of the days when the paths of the swashbuckling American mariner and the exotic Chinese craftsman crossed.

What You Need

A grown-up to assist
Layer of newspaper
Plain white oven-safe plate of any size
Pencil
Paper
Stencils (1 large design for the center and a smaller one for the rim (optional)
Tape (optional)
Blue paint pen for ceramic, glass, and tile (available in craft stores)
Sheet of moistened paper towel

What You Do

1. Lay the newspaper out on a flat surface such as the floor or a table.
2. If you choose to create your own design, make a freehand sketch with pencil and paper that you can copy. Simple designs such as butterflies, birds, flowers, shells, and boats are best. If you choose to use stencils, place a large stencil in the center of the plate. Tape it down to secure it.

3. Shake the paint pen before removing the cap. Remove the cap and press down to allow the paint to flow. Gently paint the inside space of the stencil. Be careful to reach all the edges. The paint will come out slowly at first and then more rapidly. If it comes out too quickly and your design starts to run, put the cap back on and place it aside for a minute. Lift the stencil carefully to reveal the design. A moist paper towel can clean smudges or mistakes even after the paint has dried. The paint scratches off, so you can tidy up any messy edges with your fingernail.

4. Take the smaller stencil and decorate around the plate's rim, allowing a minute or so for drying between each design. If you are drawing freehand, be careful to let each section dry as you work. When you have finished, let the plate dry for 24 hours.

5. Bake in a 300°F (148.89°C) oven for 35 minutes to set the paint.

(Note: These plates are for decorative use *only*. Do *not* use your plate for serving food.)

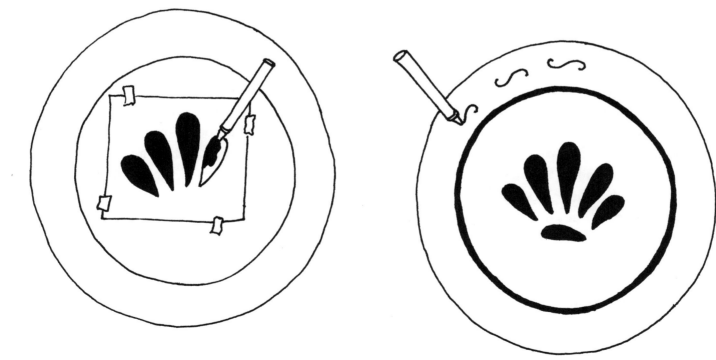

Prepare Chinese Tea

Tea accidentally became the center of America's fight for independence as well as the reason for building the famous clipper ships! In June of 1767, the British levied heavy taxes on tea to help themselves shoulder the costs of the French and Indian War. The American colonists rebelled by dressing up as Indians, sneaking onto a British ship, and tossing hundreds of pounds of tea into Boston Harbor. This was the unofficial beginning of the American Revolution.

When America won the Revolution and gained its independence, tea again became an issue. The new country began direct trade with China to import tea. In its quest to beat England to the marketplace, America built the fastest ships that had ever sailed the seas—the clippers. In the process, much was sacrificed. The clipper ships were built for this specialized market. They sacrificed cargo space for speed. The captains were very strict and bound to their schedules. They pushed both ship and crew to their limits to get the cargo into port first. They knew if they were too slow, the market would be glutted and the tea would sell for less.

What You Need

Large cup or mug

Chinese black or green tea bag

Pan or teakettle

Water

Spoon

Milk and sugar (optional)

What You Do

1. Place the teabag in the cup.
2. Heat a cup or two of water in the teakettle.
3. When the water comes to a boil, pour it into the cup and let it steep two or three minutes. (Chinese black tea actually looks reddish when it is fully brewed.)
4. Remove the teabag and place it on the spoon. Wrap the teabag's string around the spoon and gently squeeze the remaining liquid into the cup. Use caution—the teabag may still be quite hot. Discard the teabag.

Try drinking it plain like the Chinese. Drink it slowly so you can savor the smell and taste. If you like it a bit sweeter, add some milk and sugar. Enjoy!

Cook a Deliciously Sweet Bird's Nest

The Chinese considered the nests found in the caves along the cliffs of the Pacific Islands to be a delicacy. Yankee traders paid island natives to risk their lives to scale dangerous heights and retrieve these nests.

The most desirable of the nests were the mandarin nests. The second most prized were the common nests. The lowest in quality were the hairy nests. The nests were primarily made up of seaweed held together by bird saliva. Feathers and dirt were carefully removed and then the nest was boiled until it took on a gel-like consistency. The nests were most often used to make bird's-nest soup.

The delicacy of bird's-nest soup has survived to this day and is available in Asian food stores and restaurants all over the world. Here's a recipe for a different, sweeter kind of bird's nest.

What You Need

2 large cakes or 1 cup (41 grams) bite-size pieces shredded wheat cereal

2 small bowls

1 cup (about 120 grams) chocolate chips

Spoon

Milk (optional)

What You Do

1. Crumble the cereal into small strands in a bowl.
2. Pour the chocolate chips into the other bowl and microwave on high for one minute at a time until all the chocolate is melted. Stir after each minute.
3. Remove the chocolate bowl from the microwave. Be careful—it will be hot.
4. Pour the chocolate over the shredded cereal and mix it with the spoon.
5. Use your spoon to mold it into a nest shape. Let cool before eating. To make a bird's-nest soup, put the nest into a larger bowl and pour milk around it!

Yield: 1 serving

Donald McKay and His Clipper Ships

Many people think clipper ships are among the most beautiful creations ever made. With their billowing clouds of white sail, sharp concave bows, streamlined black *hulls* (ships' bodies), and sleek design, these were ships built for speed. Before the creation of clipper ships, people had assumed that if a ship was large it had to be slow as well. If speed was a consideration in a voyage, a smaller ship was used. The successful clipper ships shattered those old ideas; these were enormous vessels that could travel at lightning speed across the ocean.

Clippers were much longer than the old vessels but they were also significantly narrower. The bows were longer and sharper than any had ever been before, and their sterns sat lower in the water. The clipper sliced *through* the waves whereas the old ships' rounded bows lifted them *over* the waves. The masts were much higher and *raked*: instead of being straight, they sloped slightly aft. There was an enormous increase in the amount of sail; some clippers had five or six times as much sail as an ordinary merchantman. For 20 or so fleeting years, clipper ships ruled the seas with their majestic beauty. The pioneering builder of the most magnificent of these vessels was a man named Donald McKay.

It is said that McKay fell in love with sailing ships when, at the age of seven, he first saw a Grand Banks fishing schooner. (The Grand Banks is a 350-mile

[563.3-kilometer] underwater shelf off the coast of Newfoundland, Canada, an area known for fertile fishing grounds.) McKay spied the ship while sitting on a pile of potatoes in the back of a wagon from his father's farm in Nova Scotia. The eldest son of 16 children, Donald was a smart, curious child. As a young man he left his childhood home to fulfill his dreams in America.

At 16 he signed on as a shipwright's apprentice in New York. He worked for Isaac Webb, who became known as the father of shipbuilders because he trained so many young men who went on to build great ships. Webb soon recognized the young boy's intelligence, mechanical ability, and willingness to work hard. After four years, Webb released his apprentice so that McKay could work as a full-fledged shipwright with the shipyard Brown and Bell. McKay was 21 years old.

McKay married a shipbuilder's daughter, Albenia Martha Boole, whose own knowledge of drafting (drawing plans and designs) and mathematics helped McKay progress beyond the rudimentary education he had received in Nova Scotia. In this way, Albenia was a partner and mentor (teacher) to him. Another important relationship was with a draftsman from a neighboring shipyard named John Willis Griffiths.

The two shared innovative plans and ideas about how ships could be designed for speed.

McKay worked as a freelance (independent) shipbuilder in several yards before becoming business partners with a man named John Currier. They started the firm Currier and McKay in Newburyport, Massachusetts. They built a series of excellent packet ships during their three years together.

Shipbuilders began experimenting with a sleeker design that had a sharp, curved bow, a huge spread of sail, and slender hull. In March 1849 the *Sea Witch*, designed by McKay's friend John Willis Griffiths, made the run from Canton, China, to New York in just 74 days. Prior to this, what was considered a fast voyage would have been about 100 days.

When McKay was 34, a wealthy merchant from Boston, Enoch Train, set him up with his own shipyard in East Boston. McKay now had the freedom and authority to do things his own way. He would go on to build the fastest ships on earth. He took all the innovation of the times and applied it to his ships. From Griffiths he took the sharper bow, narrow midship, and full stern. The idea for a flatter hull came from a ship's captain named Nat Palmer.

McKay's first clipper, *Stag Hound*, was launched in 1850. At the time it was the largest merchant ship on the seas. Speed and size became essential qualities of merchant ships in the mid-1800s. The gold rush of 1849 caused thousands of people to flock to California to seek their fortunes. This created an immediate need for goods and supplies for the *prospectors* (those panning for gold). California was suffering desperate shortages of food, clothing, and dry goods. Any ship that could deliver these items quickly was destined for riches (see page 00). The other driving force spurring the design of clipper ships was the China tea trade.

On its maiden voyage in 1851, the famous *Flying Cloud*, McKay's first "extreme clipper," left New York Harbor and reached San Francisco in a record-breaking 89 days and 8 hours. A typical voyage from New York to San Francisco in the 1850s was about 200 days! A clipper from the Irons and Grinnell Shipyard in Mystic, Connecticut, the *Andrew Jackson*, broke the *Flying Cloud*'s record by four hours in 1860.

On March 18, 1853, the *Sovereign of the Seas* logged 421 nautical miles in one day on its way from New York to Honolulu, with McKay's brother, Captain Laughlin McKay, at the helm. In 1854, another of McKay's ships, the *Lightning*, traveled 436 nautical miles in one day on a voyage between Boston and Liverpool, England. Then McKay's ship

Champion of the Seas covered 465 nautical miles in one day. McKay's *James Baines* broke a transatlantic record for the Boston-to-Liverpool route, making the journey in 12 days and 6 hours.

But for all the clippers' speed and delicate beauty, the days of the ships were numbered. By about 1855 many factors were working against the clipper ship trade. Competition from the steamship caused freight charges to drop. Clippers could no longer command higher prices for the fastest delivery. The California trade had slowed down, and the shipping industry as a whole was beginning to wane. By 1860 the United States had 30,000 miles of railroad tracks, also competing to transport freight. Clippers were expensive to build and equally expensive to operate and maintain. The only opportunity left for these ships was in transporting guano and laborers. The laborers from China were enticed to the United States with promises of great opportunities; instead they found brutal, dirty working conditions and low pay. Laborers were also transported to Cuba and Australia. It was a shameful trade and a sad way to end the clipper ship era.

Many clippers were cut down and refitted to a more manageable size; others were commissioned as warships during the Civil War. In 1869 the last of the great clippers was built, Donald McKay's *Glory of the*

Seas, which had a long career that ended on May 19, 1923, when it was burned for scrap metal at Brace Point, in Seattle, Washington. The builder's model is preserved at the Mariner's Museum in Newport News, Virginia, and the figurehead of the ship is preserved at the India House in New York.

None of the American clipper ships are left (the last remaining clipper ship in the world is the British ship *Cutty Sark*, which can be seen in Greenwich, England), but their images have been captured in the art of the era, and many lovely reproductions have been built to allow us a vision of what life was like during this time. (See Resources for a listing of maritime museums that offer these reproductions.)

The launching of *Flying Cloud* at East Boston in 1851. *Peabody Essex Museum*

Lighthouses

To deepwater sailors a lighthouse was a welcome sight. It meant that land and a safe harbor were near. The lighthouse was a navigational aid that helped mariners plot their exact location as well as warned them of shallow or rocky waters and narrow harbors. Early lighthouses used oil lamps and could only be seen from a few miles out. Then a Frenchman, Augustin Fresnel, developed a special lighthouse lens that allowed the light to be seen 20 miles (32.19 kilometers) away. The *Fresnel lens* surrounds a light source with hundreds of pieces of cut glass. It forces the light, which scatters under ordinary circumstances, into a single intense beam.

Distinguishing Lighthouses

Early lighthouses were painted in different colors and designs with no particular significance attached to their appearance. As a result, navigators easily became confused when they encountered two or three lighthouses that all looked the same on a small stretch of coastline. In 1852, the Lighthouse Board, a group established by the federal government to oversee navigational aids, issued an order that each lighthouse be painted differently. Only certain color combinations can easily be seen at sea, so the colors chosen were mostly red, white, black, or a combination of those colors. Some have different patterns too, such as stripes, diamonds, or checkerboard.

These were good landmarks during the day, but at night all lighthouses still looked the same. To solve this problem the light was mounted on a rotating framework so it would appear that the light was flashing on and off. Each lighthouse was assigned a specific patterned series of these on-and-off flashes. This pattern was called the lighthouse's signature. The

Fresnel lens perfected this, allowing for thousands of flashing combinations as well as a more concentrated light. Another method of distinguishing lighthouses was through the color of the light. In addition to white lights there were green and red and combinations of these colors. The navigator had charts that listed each lighthouse's flashes and colors. With these distinctions navigators could determine their location and which lighthouse they spied.

The Lighthouse Keeper

The job of the lighthouse keeper was a very important yet solitary job. Many lighthouses were located on isolated points of land or on islands. Lighthouse keepers and their families were responsible for keeping the lamps burning even during terrible blizzards and storms. When vessels became shipwrecked along the coast, these rugged people risked their lives to row out and rescue survivors, and they offered food, clothing, and shelter as well.

The daily life of a lighthouse keeper was busy. The lamps were lit at sunset and extinguished at sunrise. Several times a night the keepers had to climb to the top of the tower to check the lamps and wind the weights, a clock type of mechanism that had to be wound every few hours. This is what made the lenses rotate in the days before electricity. Daytime meant many more hours polishing the brass, and cleaning the lens and windows so that the light could shine through brightly. The lighthouse keeper was also required to keep a daily log of weather conditions and other practical information. On foggy nights the keeper had to sound a foghorn to warn the sailors of what they could not see ahead.

Lighthouses Today

Modern lighthouses are fully automated, so lighthouse keepers are no longer needed. Boston Light, America's oldest lighthouse, in Boston Harbor, is the only one that still has a keeper, a tradition kept out of respect for its grand past. Advances in technology have made the role of the lighthouse less important. There is a government program that encourages and provides for nonprofit groups to take over the care and preservation of designated historic lighthouses. Many of these lighthouses are open to the public. They offer a wonderful way to connect with America's seafaring history. (See Resources for a listing of historic lighthouses to visit.)

Assemble a Lighthouse

ere's an easy way to make your own light-house. Making it might inspire you to write a story about life on the high seas.

What You Need

Scissors

Construction paper

Markers

Empty cardboard oatmeal container

Tape or glue

Square of removable two-sided poster mounting tape

Safety strobe light (battery-powered flashing red light that runners clip to their clothes; available in sports and hardware stores)

1-liter clear plastic soda bottle

What You Do

1. Using scissors, markers, construction paper, and tape or glue, decorate the oatmeal container to look like a lighthouse. Solid red or white, stripes, diamonds, and spirals are the most common designs.

2. Stick the mounting tape to the middle of the oatmeal cover. Press the strobe light onto the tape.

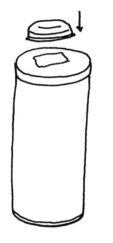

3. Cut the plastic bottle about 3 inches (7.62 centimeters) from the bottom.

4. Draw black lines with a marker on the bottle piece to make it look like metalwork. Turn the piece upside down to cover the light.

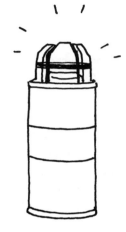

5. To light the lighthouse, remove the clear plastic bottle cover, pull the strobe light off, and push the button to turn it on. Press it back over the tape, and cover it again with the clear plastic. You should be able to see the light from up to half a mile (805 meters) away!

Abbie Burgess: Teenage Lighthouse Heroine

In January 1856, Samuel Burgess, the lighthouse keeper of Matinicus Rock, Maine, had to leave his invalid wife and four daughters to journey to the mainland. Matinicus Rock is a 32-acre (12.95 hectare) granite island located in Penobscot Bay, 18 miles (29.97 kilometers) from shore. It is about five miles (8.05 kilometers) from Matinicus Island and 25 miles (40.23 kilometers) from Rockland, the nearest port. The ship that usually brought the Burgesses' winter supplies had not come. Samuel feared that their provisions would not last through the winter. When he left, he entrusted his eldest daughter, 17-year-old Abbie, to keep the lights burning and to take care of her mother and younger sisters while he was gone.

Soon after Samuel left, a raging storm hit Matinicus Rock, and no one could land there for the next four weeks. During this time, young Abbie showed tremendous courage. Night and day she worked, clearing the ice from the windows, trimming the wicks, and filling the lamps with oil. The family's supplies dwindled until they were surviving on little more than eggs.

On the eighth day of the storm a terrible *breaker* (a wave that crashes into foam when it makes contact) more than 30 feet (9.14 meters) high hit their home. Moments before it hit, Abbie had run through knee-deep water to rescue the family hens from their coop. The breaker hit the front door of their home just after she slammed it shut, with the hens safe inside. The older, wooden part of the house completely washed away. Abbie quickly moved her mother and sisters to the lighthouse towers. Abbie said

later, "Though at times greatly exhausted by my labors, not once did the lights fail. Under God I was able to perform all my accustomed duties as well as my father's."

The ocean finally calmed in mid-February, and Samuel was able to come home. Finding his wife and children safe and the lighthouse lamps still burning, he was overcome with love and pride in his young daughter. The story of her courage soon spread, earning Abbie Burgess the title of lighthouse heroine.

Matinicus Rock Lighthouse, Maine. *United States Coast Guard*

Mutiny on the Amistad: The Story of a Slave Rebellion

A shameful part of American seafaring history was the country's participation with the Europeans in the Atlantic slave trade. From 1619 until the end of the legal transatlantic slave trade in the early 1800s, more than 8 million Africans were kidnapped and sold into slavery in the United States. Millions more perished in the holding camps along the African coast or during the journey on slave ships from Africa to America known as the *Middle Passage.*

The first leg of the transatlantic slave trade was when ships sailed from Europe with guns and manufactured goods to trade for slaves in Africa. On the second leg, or Middle Passage, slaves were brought across the Atlantic to the New World (North America, South America, and the Caribbean), where they were traded for raw materials such as sugar, molasses, tobacco, rum, and cotton. The last or third leg of the journey occurred when these New World goods were exchanged for goods to trade with the Africans for slaves.

In 1839, on a ship called the *Amistad*, African slaves rebelled and overthrew their European captors. The mutiny on the *Amistad* and the trials that followed brought the moral issue of slavery into the hearts and minds of Americans. It forced American citizens to see Africans as people, not possessions. The *Amistad* incident became a catalyst for change and led to the eventual abolition of slavery in America.

The story of the *Amistad* begins in January of 1839, when Spanish slave traders purchased Africans from native kidnappers in West Africa. They held the captives in temporary camps along the coast called *barracoons* before secretly loading them into ships bound for the New World. They had to be careful because at this point in history, capturing new slaves was illegal, and British ships patrolled the coast to arrest anyone involved in the slave trade.

A group of 53 men, women, and children was led in chains to the ship *Tecora*. There they were stripped naked and hosed down before being squeezed onto the filthy deck. The hold of the deck was only three feet high, and there was not even enough room to turn without touching another person. They had to relieve their bladders and bowels right where they lay. They were only allowed on deck once a day. For weeks they suffered illness, floggings, and near starvation. At last the ship sailed into Havana, Cuba, in June of 1839.

In Cuba, the slaves were led under cover of darkness to a new barracoon, where 49 of the captives were resold to Spaniards Jose Ruiz and Pedro Montez. The Spaniards and their human cargo shipped out on a new ship, the *Amistad*. Desperation was beginning to set in among the captives. Their rations had been cut. When some of them tried to eat more than their share, they were brutally flogged.

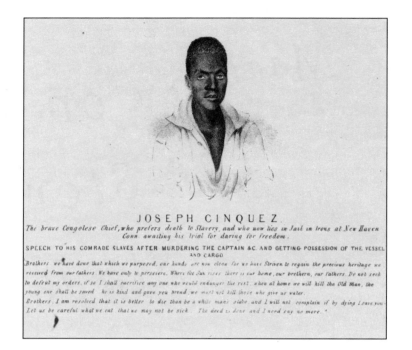

The caption of this photo reads, "Joseph Cinquez. The brave Congolese Chief, who prefers death to Slavery, and who now lies in Jail in Irons at New Haven Conn. awaiting his trial for daring for freedom." The publisher of the *New York Sun* newspaper commissioned this portrait. It was published and advertised for sale in that newspaper's August 31, 1839, issue. *Library of Congress*

The ship's cook pantomimed (nonverbally communicated) to the slaves that they were going to be eaten.

A brave rice farmer named Sengbe Pieh, called Cinqué by the Spaniards, conceived a daring plan to take over the ship. He believed if they could free enough men from their chains, they could overthrow the slave traders with machetes that they had seen onboard. Cinqué had become friends with another strong, proud captive named Grabeau, who agreed to the plan. A prisoner named Burna, who had been a blacksmith in Africa, figured out that the shackles on their hands operated with a spring mechanism.

On the third night out, there was a storm. The captives decided to seize their opportunity while the crew was distracted. One by one they worked feverishly with a nail to unlock the shackles. In rapid succession, each prisoner unlocked the chains of the next until enough men had been freed to strike. They crashed onto the deck without warning and attacked the crew. The captain was the first to be killed, followed by the cook. One African was killed during the fight, and two crew members either escaped by boat or died during the attack.

The Africans allowed Jose Ruiz and Pedro Montez to remain alive to navigate the ship. The cabin boy was also spared because he could act as an interpreter between the Spaniards and the Africans. The slaves ordered the Spaniards to steer the ship east, back to Africa. During the day, when the Africans could tell the direction of the sun, the Spaniards sailed east, but at night and on cloudy days they sailed west to stay within Cuban waters. Seven more Africans died on the journey. Exhausted and depleted of food and water supplies, the Africans decided to row into Long Island, New York, to replenish them. It was there that the Africans were placed back in chains and arrested as mutineers.

The Spaniards produced forged documents from Cuba saying that the slaves were Cuban-born legal slaves, instead of illegal African slaves. (Importing new slaves had been illegal in America since 1808.) The Africans found themselves in a country deeply divided by the issue of slavery. Many states, especially in the North, had banned slavery, but many Southern states depended on slaves to work on large cotton plantations. Abolitionists, people who were morally opposed to the institution of slavery and worked to abolish it, put together a legal team to defend the Africans.

The Africans were held as prisoners through a series of trials until the court of New Haven, Connecticut, proclaimed them to be free Africans and not legal Cuban slaves. The judge ordered that the United States return them to Africa. In a cruel twist, the president of the United States, Martin Van Buren, concerned about his own political future, made the disgraceful decision to have the case overturned and sent to the Supreme Court. Former president John Quincy Adams joined the abolitionists' cause, masterfully arguing the Africans' case before the Supreme Court. The court agreed that the

Africans had been illegally enslaved and had a right to their freedom.

This time the court decided that the United States was not responsible for the Africans' passage back to Africa. Private funds from religious and abolitionist groups eventually secured passage for the 35 surviving Africans and various missionaries aboard the ship *Gentleman*. They finally arrived home in Sierra Leone, Africa, in January of 1842.

Sadly, Cinqué and many of the other *Amistad* captives returned to find that their families had been killed in war or sold into slavery. The missionaries opened the Mendi Mission at Komende, near Freetown, Sierra Leone. The original plan was that the *Amistad* passengers would stay together, but most of the Africans eventually scattered and returned to traditional African life. One of the child captives, Margru Kinson, later went to Oberlin College in the United States and returned to Africa as a missionary.

There are conflicting stories about what happened to Joseph Cinqué (Sengbe Pieh). Some say that he left with goods to trade in another area and never came back; others say that he left but eventually returned to the mission, where he died.

Play the Morse Code Signal Game

Beginning in the 1840s, deepwater sailors sent messages to other ships using a special communication code. *Morse code* is a series of dots and dashes that represent letters and numbers. Ships sent these messages with a lamp device called a heliograph that worked by reflecting the sun with mirrors. Later the heliograph was replaced by an electric lamp known as an Aldis lamp.

Morse code can be communicated in many ways. It can be transmitted by telegraph (an apparatus that sends messages by code over wires), through radio transmissions—it has a distinctive *dit* for dot and *dah* for dash—and many other ways, such as through tapping, foghorn sounds, and by whistles.

Using a flashlight, send a message to a friend in Morse code.

What You Need

1 or more flashlights
The international Morse code (below)

A	• _	K	_ • _	U	• • _
B	_ • • •	L	• _ • •	V	• • • _
C	_ • _ •	M	_ _	W	• _ _
D	_ • •	N	_ •	X	_ • • _
E	•	O	_ _ _	Y	_ • _ _
F	• • _ •	P	• _ _ •	Z	_ _ • •
G	_ _ •	Q	_ _ • _		
H	• • • •	R	• _ •		
I	• •	S	• • •		
J	• _ _ _	T	_		

What You Do

1. Before starting this activity, learn these signaling rules.

   A dash is always equal in time to three dots.

   A space between dots and dashes takes the same amount of time as a dot.

   A space between words takes the same time as five dots.

2. Think of a well-known nautical phrase such as "clear the decks."

3. Using Morse code, turn the flashlight on and off for each dash or dot. Keep the flashlight on three seconds for each dash and one second for each dot. Wait one second between each dash or dot. Wait five seconds between each word. It takes some practice!

If you find it easier to go more slowly, keep the flashlight on for six seconds for each dash and two seconds for each dot. Wait two seconds between each dash or dot. Wait ten seconds between each word.

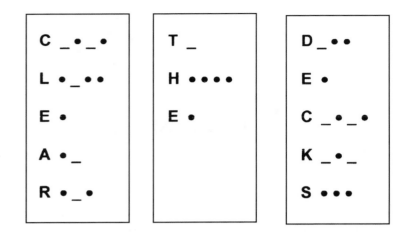

C _ • _ •
L • _ • •
E •
A • _
R • _ •

T _
H • • • •
E •

D _ • •
E •
C _ • _ •
K _ • _
S • • •

Marlinspike: Making Sailor's Knots

The first skill a boy learned aboard ship was how to tie knots. An improperly tied line could result in death for a sailor 100 feet (30.48 meters) up on a mast. A *marlinspike sailor* was a master at tying knots; this nickname stemmed from the tool by that name that separates rope. Marlinspike handiwork was respected for its utility as well as its decorative properties. These knots secured sails, yards, and masts. Decorative knots that hung from ship's bells, sea chests, and ditty bags were also known as *fancywork*. The old salts took great pride in sharing their marlinspike skills with the greenhands. Many an hour was spent in the fo'c'sle working and reworking a star knot or a monkey's fist.

There are several thousand types of knots. Seamen categorize them into knots, bends, hitches, and splices. A knot occurs when a rope goes through a loop made by itself. Two major types are stopper knots and binding knots. Stopper knots can prevent a rope from fraying or from slipping through a hole; they are also used as handholds. Binding knots are used for tying things up and are fixed in place. A bend is used to join two ropes. Hitches join a rope to an object. A splice is made by unraveling two ropes at the ends and interweaving them to make a new rope.

Once a rope has a function aboard ship, it is named and known as a line. For example, *halyards* are lines because they are ropes used for hoisting sails and yards. A jib sheet is a line because it controls the position of the jib sail. A footrope is also a line because sailors use it to stand on while setting sails. A rope sitting in a bucket is a rope, not a line, because it doesn't have a specific purpose.

Try tying a knot, a bend, and a hitch.

What You Need

2 3-foot (.914-meter) lengths of any rope, about ½ inch (1.27 centimeters) in diameter

What You Do

Follow the diagrams to make each of these knots.

Figure-Eight Knot

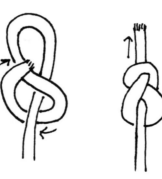

This is a seaman's stopper knot. It is used to keep a line from running through a block, and as a stopper at the end of running rigging.

Sheet Bend

This is the most common general-purpose bend used in sailing. It is also used to join two ropes of different widths.

Two Half Hitches

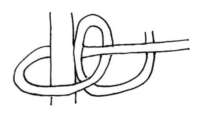

This knot attaches a line to a pole or ring. It is used to hook up to a mooring, to make a sling for lifting a cask, and for general purposes.

Packet Ships

Can you imagine how frustrating it would be to plan a trip if when your flight was supposed to leave, the pilot told you to come back when the cargo area was full or when he had more passengers or when it was a sunny day? That's what it was like for passengers traveling across the ocean during the first two centuries of life in America. Sailing dates were ignored as captains waited days or even weeks to fill their holds or for bad weather to clear before they departed. Finally in 1817, a group of resourceful New York merchants did something about the need for reliable ocean travel. They started the Black Ball Line, a fleet of ships that was the first to sail on a timetable between New York and Liverpool. The ships would transport mail, cargo, and most importantly, passengers.

Several packet lines followed, including routes to London and Le Havre, France. They all used the same guidelines: the ship left on time and arrived at its destination on time whether full or empty, in good weather or bad. Packet ships evolved into their own design, a cross between a clipper ship (which could cut quickly through the water) and a frigate (which had plenty of cargo space). A trip from New York to Liverpool cost about $125, a sum that only the rich could afford at the time. The quarters were luxurious, with carved polished wood and pampering by stewards who waited on guests and served full-course meals. Although the passengers traveled in luxury, it was still a tedious and often uncomfortable voyage, averaging 24 days en route to England and 38 days home. The difference in time on the return voyage allowed for prevailing westerly winds. It was described as sailing downhill to the east and uphill to the west.

Packet ship captains were the most respected in their profession. They had to be highly skilled, able to make quick decisions, and brave. They had to push the limits of the crew and the ship to meet strict timetables. The ships carried much more sail than other ships, and often the crew had to work through ice and storms to stay on schedule. If the wind were rising, more prudent captains would *shorten sail* (reduce or take in a part of the sail). The packet ship captains, bent on speed, would press on. If a sailing ship was carrying a lot of sail and hit a squall or gale, it was at the sea's mercy because sails can rip and fly away, and ships can capsize. This is a risky way to sail. Despite these pressures, the captain was also responsible for the safety of the people and cargo onboard.

Typical American exports on packet ships were cotton, grain, cheese, and tobacco. Imports included European textiles, crockery, wine, iron, steel, and a variety of manufactured goods.

Soon competition squeezed the market for cargo to be transported back to America, and a new market emerged in the mid-1800s that coincided with European emigration. This was a category for inexpensive passenger travel known as *steerage*. The packet ships packed the in-between decks with hundreds of people who were leaving their homelands for opportunities in America. Most left with little but the clothes on their back and a small amount of food.

They paid about $20 per person for passage and endured a miserable and sometimes deadly voyage.

Between 1846 and 1855, more than two million people made the journey across the Atlantic to America. Steerage travelers had to cope with crowded conditions with as many as 500 passengers, compared to 20 or 30 in first class. Passengers suffered seasickness; diseases such as cholera, smallpox, and typhus; lack of decent food and fresh water; damp, dark, and wet quarters; and lack of ventilation and fresh air. The sleeping berths were so close together that there wasn't even enough room to sit up in bed. The stench of the steerage deck was sickening; a combination of bilge water from the holds of the ship, vomit, slop buckets overflowing with urine and feces, and stale air.

Steerage passengers were responsible for bringing and cooking most of their food, a practice that was forbidden by law but ignored by most captains. The makeshift stoves were dangerous, basically just brick stacks with grates over the top. Because the ship was so crowded, people had to wait in line for hours to cook their food. As the ship pitched, it was a struggle to prevent the food from sliding away. Entire meals were wasted and people suffered burns from the hot liquids. If the weather was bad, they weren't allowed to use the stoves at all.

This was quite a contrast to the conditions of the first-class passengers above who spent their days playing shuffleboard, listening to orchestral music, and dining on roast chicken and wine from the ship's galley.

Competition from steamship lines began in 1838 and continued until the last of the packet ships made its final run in May of 1881. The ship's prophetic name, *Ne Plus Ultra*, means "Nothing Further."

Our next chapter takes us on liberty—the free time sailors enjoyed while a ship was in port. The sailor became America's first ambassador to many foreign ports. In some of the more isolated islands, the natives had never seen a white man before.

Emigrant ship, between decks, 1850. *Peabody Essex Museum*

131

4
Land Ho! Foreign Ports

Come with us on liberty! Relax in Honolulu with a flower garland and a plate of baked bananas. Try making a feather cape similar to the ones the Hawaiian kings wore. Witness the colorful sights of Canton when you make a Chinese junk and dragon boat, then trade for an Inuit mask and make a sailor's valentine for someone you love at home.

Wine, women, and song! That's what the sailor sought when his ship pulled into port. But the shipmaster's reasons for anchoring in a foreign port had to do with business. He was there to replenish provisions, make repairs, or trade goods. Yankee ships stopped at tropical Pacific islands, bustling European cities, exciting South American ports, and exotic eastern harbors in Japan, China, India, and Australia.

Liberty, sweet liberty, was freedom for the sailor, who had been at sea for weeks or months under the tight control of the captain and his officers. The sailor wanted to drown out all the suffering of the voyage—the poor food, wet clothing, harsh discipline, crowded quarters, and grinding work—with as much pleasure as he could stuff into 24 or 48 hours. In 1840, Liverpool, England, the most visited of all sailor towns, had more than 2,000 taverns.

Seaport towns thrived on the appetites of the childlike sailor. Adept and brave at sea, the sailor was sometimes the opposite on land, where he was often taken advantage of. *Land sharks* were people who made a living by charging sailors extra-high prices for hotel rooms, meals, tavern drinks, clothing, tattoos, and dance hall admission. Soon the sailor ended up back on ship, drunk, broke, and often sporting a few cuts and scrapes from a barroom brawl.

The worst parasite in waterfront towns was the *crimp*. The crimp stalked sailors on behalf of other ships in need of crewmembers. He would pretend to be a friend, get the sailor drunk, and then persuade him to sign papers binding him to a voyage at sea. The ship's captain paid the crimp out of the sailor's future wages. This practice could keep a sailor broke and in debt for years.

Not all sailors ended up in trouble. Many went sightseeing; sought out places of worship; and engaged in recreational activities such as horseback riding, bowling, and swimming. If a captain had his family onboard, they visited with other seafaring families or local dignitaries in port. They enjoyed gossip from home and the best of local food and

Wharf in Auckland, New Zealand, August 11, 1908. *Library of Congress*

entertainment. Journals from sea captain's wives abound with stories of watching the natives dance in Tahiti, eating fresh pineapple in Honolulu, and visiting Napoleon's grave in St. Helena.

Many sailors deserted (abandoned their ship) at these foreign ports. Some lingered on beaches in warm Pacific isles or joined the crew aboard another ship. Shipmasters dealt with this in different ways. If native crew (crewmen from the islands) were plentiful, it saved him money, but if they were scarce, a deserting sailor could be arrested and forced back onto the ship. Eventually the ship returned to sea until "Land Ho!" rang out again.

Make a Maori Grass Skirt

New Zealand, especially the Bay of Islands, was a popular port of call for Yankee ships. The Maori are the native Polynesian people in New Zealand. The traditional Maori garment, the piupiu, is painstakingly woven from hundreds of blades of flax into a skirt and decorated with thick brown stripes made from a mud stain. It is worn by men and women alike, usually with a red underskirt. Red is considered a tapu (sacred) color in Maori culture.

What You Need

10 yards (9.14 meters) of red ribbon 1½ inches (3.81 centimeters) wide

Cloth tape measure

Scissors

Pen

Aluminum foil

75–100 yards (68.58–91.44 meters) of light tan raffia ribbon. (Note: Raffia ribbon is a type of imitation raffia that is easier to work with than natural raffia, which comes in strands. The more you use, the fuller the skirt will be.)

Fabric or craft glue

Plastic bowl or plate

Heavy books to place over the skirt while it dries

Brown acrylic paint and paintbrush to make stripes (optional)

Red skirt or red shorts

What You Do

1. Measure (or have a friend help you measure) your waist with the red ribbon, and then add 1 foot (30.48 centimeters) on either side to tie it. Cut.

2. Mark the waist area on the ribbon with a pen. Lay the ribbon flat over some aluminum foil. (If you use newspaper as your work surface the skirt will stick.)

3. Cut a second piece of red ribbon the size of your waist area plus 1 inch (2.54 centimeters) on each side—for a total of 2 inches (5.08 centimeters) longer—and set aside.

4. Cut the raffia ribbon into strips that measure from your waist to just below your knee.

5. Pour the glue into a nonporous container such as a plastic bowl or plate.

6. Dip the ends of each piece of raffia into the glue, one at a time, and press down on the longer red ribbon. This is time-consuming but not difficult. It is better to use too much glue than too little.

7. Now take the second piece of red ribbon and cover it with glue. Press over the first ribbon, so that the raffia is in the middle of the two pieces of red ribbon.

8. Place a piece of aluminum foil over the glued areas and place heavy books on top until they dry.

9. If you like, you can paint thick brown stripes over the raffia. Let dry. Wear the skirt over a red skirt or red shorts.

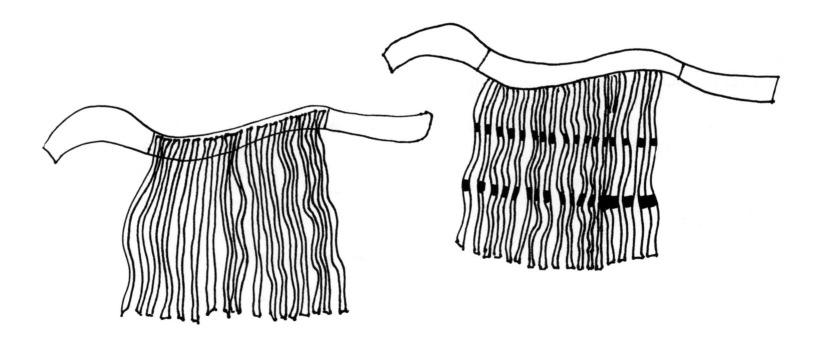

Create an English Pedlar Doll

(Note: *Pedlar* is an older spelling of the word *peddler*.)

A popular gift for the lucky daughter of a sea captain was a doll from a foreign port. The most lavish were called fashion dolls and reflected the latest in European fashion. They were delicate, painted porcelain or wooden dolls with real hair, gold earrings, and pearl-studded silk dresses. Interestingly, many little girls found the more homely pedlar dolls from England more appealing. The English called them notion nannies because they were modeled after the old women who sold housewares in the English countryside. The pedlar doll had a shallow basket around her waist filled with miniature pots and pans, thread, knitting needles, wool, wax, quills (for writing), and other household items. These dolls with their miniature wares were more fun to play with than the fragile fashion dolls.

Here's how you can make one for yourself.

What You Need

8½-inch (21.59-centimeter) by 11-inch (27.94-centimeter) piece of red felt (for cape)

Paper

Pen

Scissors

Hole punch

8½-inch (21.59-centimeter) by 11-inch (27.94-centimeter) piece of white felt (for apron)

11-inch (27.94-centimeter) doll with simple dress (Note: This is not a baby doll. If you don't have one, you can buy an inexpensive one at a craft store.)

2-foot (60.96-centimeter) strand of yarn

Heavy-duty white thread

3-inch (7.62-centimeter) basket (available at craft stores)

Miscellaneous miniature household items for basket

What You Do

1. Place the sheet of paper on top of the doll pattern and trace. Cut out these patterns.
2. Fold the red felt in half and trace around the cape pattern with the pen, lining up the left side of the pattern with the fold.
3. Cut through both layers of the felt, then punch a hole through both layers, and unfold.
4. Fold the white felt in half, and trace around the apron pattern with the pen, lining up the left side of the pattern with the fold.
5. Cut through both layers, then punch a hole through both layers, and unfold.
6. Put the apron around the doll's neck and tie behind with a 6-inch (15.24-centimeter) piece of yarn.
7. Pull the cape over the doll's head and shoulders and tie in front with a 6-inch (15.24-centimeter) piece of yarn.
8. Pull pieces of thread through two or three places in the basket and tie around the doll's waist and neck.
9. Use your imagination in filling up the pedlar doll's basket. You can use dollhouse miniatures, toy tea sets, toy dishes, tiny rolled-up balls of yarn, felt cut to look like wool, tiny scraps of cotton fabric, birthday candles cut to miniature size, and feathers cut to look like tiny quills.

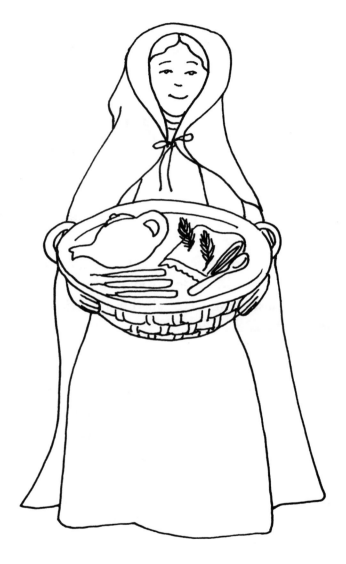

Apron pattern

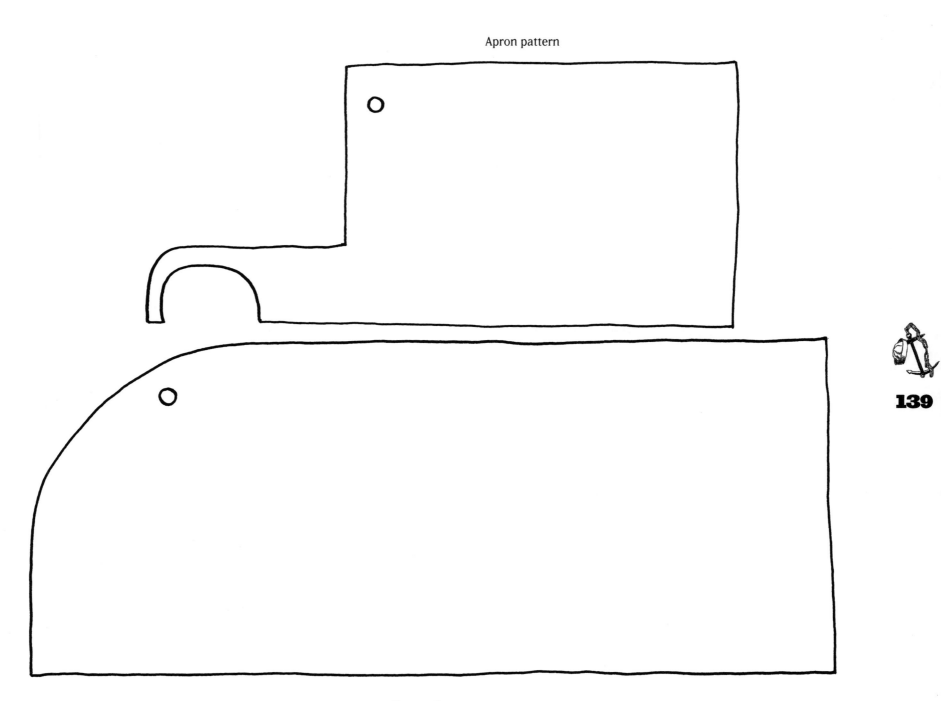

Cape pattern

Craft an Inuit Mask

The Inuit are native people of the Arctic Circle, where the Yankee whalers hunted. Whalemen as well as merchants traded with the Inuit, who sometimes were invited to sign up for duty with American whaling crews. *Inuit* means the people; it is the name they call themselves. Another name you may have heard them called is *Eskimo*; this is a name given to them by the Algonquian Indians, and it means "eater of raw meat." During the age of sail, Inuits derived most of their vitamins and minerals from eating the raw blubber of sea animals, as the climate was too cold to grow fruits and vegetables. These native people were excellent whale, seal, and walrus hunters who chased their prey from open wood-frame boats called umiaks.

The Inuit lived close to nature in the harsh climate of the Arctic, where temperatures regularly dip many degrees below zero and the sun does not shine for months at a time in winter. Before the Inuit killed an animal, they felt that the animal must agree to be killed. They respected the animal's spirit and did not waste any part of its remains. Every piece was put to use, fur for clothing, teeth for amulets (charms), meat for food, walrus hides for boats, and oil for lamps.

During whaling season all noisy work, such as chopping or pounding, was avoided as this might offend the whale. Once a whale was slaughtered, the Inuit followed a solemn ritual. First a messenger or runner delivered the tip of the whale's right flipper to the wife of the man responsible for the kill, and they shared some of the meat that he delivered. Then the wife dressed herself in new sealskin clothing made especially for the occasion. Next, she carried an ax and water as she led a procession of villagers to the whale.

The wife cut off the snout, eyes, and blowhole of the whale. Next she poured water over them and into the umiak, thanking the whale for its gifts. Her husband did the same and asked the whale to come back in the spring.

Finally the whale was cut up. Ritual dictated that the heart and flippers went to the boat header. Then the entire community joined in to cut and carry the whale's flesh and bone to the camp on sleds. The Inuit truly lived, worked, and shared as a community, and the slaughter of a whale meant food for everyone. They believed that by following these respectful ceremonies, they had properly honored the whale's spirit, and that it would return to them in the body of another whale.

The Inuit used masks for special ceremonies led by a shaman, a community's priest or priestess, to pay respect to the animal's spirit. Sailors brought some of these masks home, where they were admired as exotic treasures.

You can make your own Inuit-style mask. Masks of animals were common and were sometimes crafted as half-animal/half-human to show the respectful relationship between the two. Choose an animal that the Inuit hunted: whale, seal, walrus, caribou, or fox.

What You Need

A grown-up to assist
Pen
Paper
1 sheet of newspaper
1 roll of plaster cloth (This is a special type of cloth that has been pretreated with plaster. You can find it in craft stores.)
Scissors
Paper cup half filled with warm water
Inexpensive plastic mask (available at craft or costume stores)
Acrylic paint
Paintbrush
Decoration: Feathers, color-coated wire, pipe cleaners, felt, beads, and yarn
Hot glue gun or glue

What You Do

1. Draw an animal or animal/human mask to copy.
2. Cut strips of plaster cloth, dip them one at a time in water, and place them back and forth across the mask four or five layers deep. Try to let each strip drip a bit over the cup first. Press each piece down firmly. (*Do not pour the water down the drain.* It will harden and cause problems with the pipes. Instead, stuff a newspaper or paper towel into what's left in the paper cup and throw it away.)
3. Let the mask dry overnight.
4. Remove the plastic mask underneath. Paint the plaster using your earlier drawing as a guide.
5. Let it dry.

6. An adult should use the glue gun to help you decorate with feathers, yarn, and more. Be careful not to
   touch the tip of the glue gun because it will be very
   hot. You may use ordinary glue if you wish, but it
   will take longer to dry. Let the mask dry completely
   before you pick it up again.

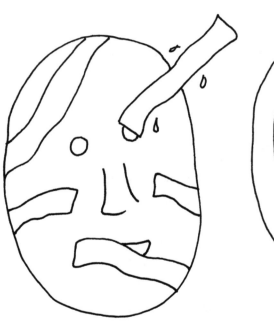

Play with Tangrams

Sailors brought countless Chinese games, toys, and puzzles back to America during the old China trade. The tangram was a popular puzzle that originated in China. An old Chinese folktale says that a man named Tan dropped a square piece of tile that he was carrying and it broke into seven pieces. When he knelt down to pick them up, he thought the pieces were forming pictures. He got so involved designing birds, trees, butterflies, and other silhouettes that he forgot why he had been carrying the tile.

The tangram is a square cut into seven geometric shapes, or tans. The tans can be combined to create animals, geometric shapes, buildings, people, and more. The rules are that you must use all the pieces, they must lie flat, they must touch, and they must not overlap.

The Chinese made tangrams from many different materials, such as pottery, ivory, and even jade. Here is a tangram you can make out of paper or foam.

What You Need

Tracing paper (or photocopy the tangram puzzle from the book)
Marker
1 8-by-10-inch (20.32-centimeter-by-25.4-centimeter) piece of heavyweight paper or 2-millimeter-thick foam sheet, any color
Pencil
Scissors

What You Do

1. Trace the tangram puzzle onto a piece of tracing paper with the marker (or use a photocopy).
2. Place the paper over the foam or heavyweight paper and make indentations along the lines with your pencil.
3. Go over the indentations with marker.
4. Cut into pieces along the lines.

Follow the basic tangram rules: use all pieces, no overlapping, touch on at least one side.

Try solving these tangrams. You'll find them easy when the lines are included. (Answers are on page 147.)

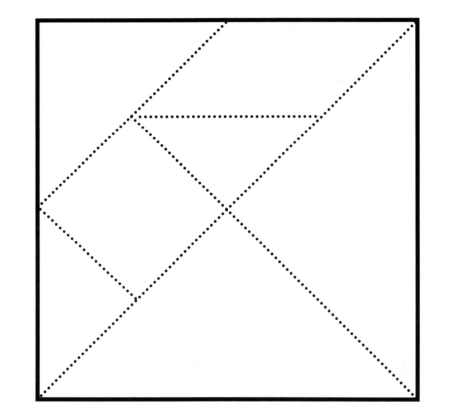

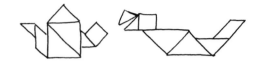

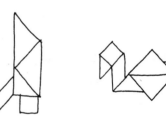

Now try solving these tangrams without the lines. They're quite a challenge!

Candle

Boat

Whale

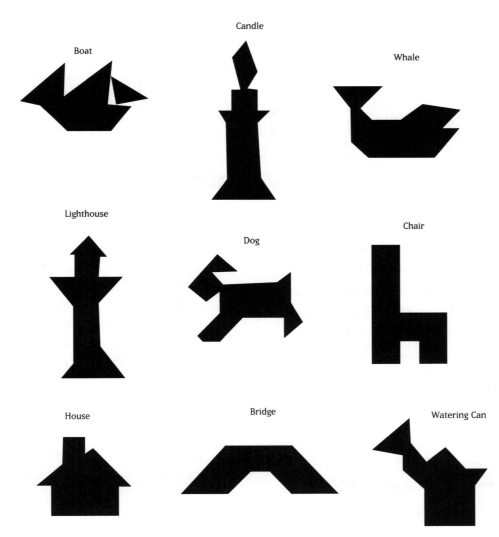

Lighthouse

Dog

Chair

House

Bridge

Watering Can

Pretend to Carve a Soapstone Whale

ailors brought home many soapstone carvings from their foreign travels. Soapstone carving is practiced all over the world, but it is a primary art form for the Inuit and Chinese. Soapstone is a rock principally made up of talc, a soft mineral with a soapy, greasy feel to it. This softness makes it an easy material to carve. It ranges in color from grayish white to grayish green.

What You Need

A grown-up to assist
Paper towel work surface
Aluminum foil for base
8 ounces (226.8 grams) white polymer clay
Toothpicks for carving
Glass ovenproof dish

What You Do

1. Preheat the oven to 275°F (135°C).
2. Lay out a few sheets of paper towel to cover your work surface.
3. Make a 3-by-1-inch (7.62-by-2.54-centimeter) loglike ball of foil. Twist it so that the ends are tapered similar to a banana. This will be the body of the whale. Make the same type of loglike shape with a 3-by-½-inch (7.62-by-1.27-centimeter) piece to make the tail.
4. Bend in the middle to flip up.
5. Take a small amount of clay and knead it in your hands until it is easy to work with. Cover the aluminum body with ¼ to ½ inch (6.35 to 12.7

millimeters) of clay. Do the same with the tail and attach the two. Make two small flippers for the sides and attach.

6. Use the toothpick to carve eyes on either side of the head, a mouth, and lines for markings underneath the belly.

7. Place the whale in the glass dish and place in the oven. Bake 15 minutes for every ¼ inch (6.35 millimeters) of thickness. (This piece should take about 30 minutes. If you want to change the way it looks after baking, you can still carve, sand, and paint the hardened clay.)

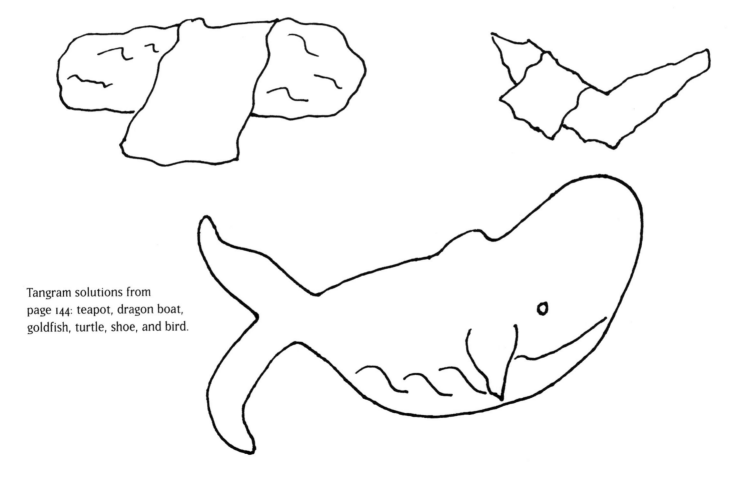

Tangram solutions from page 144: teapot, dragon boat, goldfish, turtle, shoe, and bird.

Honolulu and Lahaina

Paradise! That's what these Pacific islands must have seemed like to the weary Yankee whalemen after months at sea. Honolulu and Lahaina in the Hawaiian Islands (then called the Sandwich Islands) were favorite ports in the Pacific to rest, mend sails and rigging, replenish supplies, make repairs, and replace crew with well-respected native seafarers called kanakas.

What a contrast going from the stinking hulk of the whaler—with its dark, crowded fo'c'sle, salt junk meals, foul water, and four-hour watches—to the grass huts, gentle breezes, bountiful flowers and fruits, and crystal water of the islands. In the early years, a sailor's first introduction to the island was the wahines, native women who swam up naked to meet the Yankee ships. Missionaries, in their quest to bring what they believed was a moral way of life to the islands, soon put an end to this practice.

From the early 1800s on, there was an inevitable clashing between the missionaries—religious people who settled in the islands to spread the teachings of Christianity—and sailors who were in search of constant merriment. While the missionaries passed out Bibles and preached temperance (no alcohol consumption) from the pulpit, sailors filled the grog shops (taverns) of Lahaina. And as sailors frolicked with grass-skirted natives, missionaries worked to clothe the women in "Mother Hubbard" dresses, which they deemed more appropriate attire for proper Christians. These dresses were long-sleeved, loose gowns that covered the body. The style eventually evolved into the familiar, brightly flowered Hawaiian muumuu.

A View of Karakakooa in Owhyhee, from Cook's voyage.
Library of Congress

Honolulu and Lahaina eventually became ports where merchant ships and whalers formed their own trade route. Rather than sailing all the way home with a full ship of whale oil and bone, a whaler could sell its products in Honolulu or Lahaina to merchant ships that were in need of cargo. This allowed the whaler to continue on to the whaling grounds near Japan or the Arctic for another load of oil and bone.

Captain James Cook

Captain James Cook was a British navigator and explorer who made three geographically significant voyages around the world under the sponsorship of the British navy. He essentially mapped out the vast Pacific Ocean, including the Sandwich Islands (which we now call Hawaii). He was remarkably accurate in his chartings due to the fact that he used a new type of clock known as a *chronometer*, which measured longitude. His three voyages were aboard two ships—*Endeavour* (1768–1771) and *Resolution* (1772–1775 and 1776–1779).

Cook took an astronomer, botanists, and artists along on these voyages. They assisted him in making astronomical observations and in recording the wildlife and plants of the islands. Captain Cook was the first shipmaster to see the connection between eating fruits and vegetables and preventing scurvy, a dangerous and common disease among sailors that was caused by a vitamin deficiency. He fed his crew daily rations of sauerkraut, limes, and lemons.

In 1799 he returned to Kealakekua Bay (Hawaii), where throngs of admiring natives greeted him. Events took an unexpected turn when natives stole one of Cook's boats. Cook tried to get the offenders to return it by capturing the chief and holding him hostage. A skirmish ensued during which Cook shot one of the natives. Admiration changed to rage and Cook was murdered by the mob.

Ambrosia:
Fruits of Paradise

The whaleman at sea went for weeks and sometimes months without fruits and vegetables. If he was lucky he might have a handful of raisins in a plum duff or a stray carrot in the stew. When the ship finally anchored at one of the Pacific islands, groves of pineapple, banana, and coconut trees beckoned to the sailors. Ambrosia is a combination of traditional Pacific fruits that sailors and seagoing families enjoyed.

Over the course of the 19th century, Honolulu and Lahaina came to resemble New England towns. Ships delivered goods from home, and shipmasters and their families settled in for weeks and months at a time. Captains left for the Arctic or the Pacific and returned for their families on the way home. Seagoing families had picnics, went horseback riding, and visited back and forth. In their peak year, 1846, there were 596 visits to the islands from whaleships.

Make a Chinese Junk

With their flat bottoms and square bows, Chinese junks may be the oldest form of sailing vessel. The sails are rectangular brown canvas with horizontal bamboo battens, which strengthen and flatten the sail. Their majestic beauty must have been quite a spectacle to the young sailors from New England.

What You Need

A grown-up to assist
Pen
2 sponges
Glue
1 dowel ¼-inch-(6.35 millimeters) diameter and 26 inches (66.04 centimeters) long, cut with a small coping saw or knife into 4 pieces of the following lengths: 5 inches (12.7 centimeters), 6 inches (15.25 centimeters), 7 inches (17.78 centimeters), and 8 inches (20.32 centimeters).
Ruler
Brown paper grocery bag
Scissors
Stapler
2 heavy books
Toothpicks
Hole punch

What You Do

To Make the Boat Frame

1. Use the pen to poke two holes in each sponge to secure the dowels.
2. Fill the holes with glue and press the dowels inside.
3. From the grocery bag, cut out a rectangle 12 inches (30.48 centimeters) long by 6 inches (15.24 centimeters) wide for the bottom of the boat.
4. Fold each end in about 3 inches (7.62 centimeters), making a triangle, as though wrapping a gift. Pull the tip of the triangle up and staple as indicated in the illustration. Fold the tip away from the boat.

5. Now glue the sponges with dowels attached side by side inside the boat bottom, making a square.

6. Glue the sides of the sponges. Press them together to make them adhere.

7. Sandwich the boat between two heavy books and let dry.

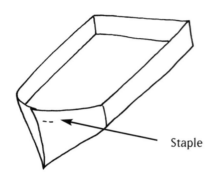

Staple

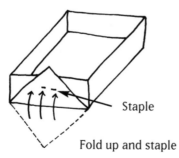

Staple

Fold up and staple

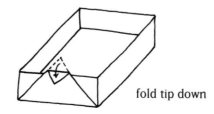

fold tip down

To Make the Sails

1. Cut out four rectangles from the bag. The width should be as long as your toothpicks and the lengths should be 4 inches (10.16 centimeters), 5 inches (12.7 centimeters), 6 inches (15.24 centimeters), and 7 inches (17.78 centimeters).

2. Using the hole punch, make a hole in the middle of the top and the middle of the bottom of each sail.

3. Fold each sail into accordion pleats about 1 inch (2.54 centimeters) apart, then open.

4. Glue a toothpick into each crease on both sides. Let dry.

To Make the Deck

1. Cut out 4 1-inch (2.54-centimeter) squares from the bag.

2. Punch a hole in the middle of each and slip one square over each dowel.

3. Cut out 1-inch (2.54-centimeter) strips in various lengths so that you cover the sponges.

4. Glue the paper down.

5. Slip the sails over the dowels. Sail away!

Create a Dragon Boat

One of the first sights the American seafarer in China saw was the colorful dragon boat. These boats have been used for hundreds of years for fishing and transportation. They are long, sleek canoe-like vessels made of teak wood and rowed by paddlers sitting side by side. In China the dragon is a symbol of power, success, and all things good.

China has celebrated the dragon boat festival for more than 2,400 years. It commemorates Qu Yuan, a poet who was an adviser to Emperor Huai of the Chu state. When the Chu state was in conflict with the Qin state. Qu Yuan was a valuable consultant, and his high status with the emperor made the other officials jealous. They devised a plot against him. They told the emperor that Qu Yuan was not to be trusted, and the weak king believed their stories and sent Qu Yuan into exile. The poet became a wanderer. During this time he wrote many of his greatest poems. When Qu Yuan found out that his beloved Chu state had been taken over by the Qin state, he drowned himself in the Mei Lo River.

Legend claims that because Qu Yuan was a respected man, fishermen in dragon boats raced to throw rice dumplings into the river to keep the fish from eating his body. Today dragon boat races are held all over the world.

What You Need

Paper
Pen
Brown grocery bag
Scissors
Stapler
Colored pencils, markers, or crayons
Construction paper

What You Do

1. Trace the dragon boat bottom from page 155 using paper and pen.
2. Cut out pattern.
3. Place the pattern on top of the grocery bag and cut out.
4. Fold along middle.
5. Pinch the 2 paper edges on 1 side and curl in toward the middle of the paper. Staple edges together close to the edge. Repeat on the other side.
6. Trace or copy the dragon boat design 2 times from page 156.
7. Color the dragons.
8. Staple to the sides of the boat.
9. Decorate the boat.

Sampan

The *sampan* is another Chinese boat that has been used since before Westerners traded with China. It is usually brightly painted and full of people who have items for sale. Sampans are still used for transport and houseboat living along China's rivers and coastal waters.

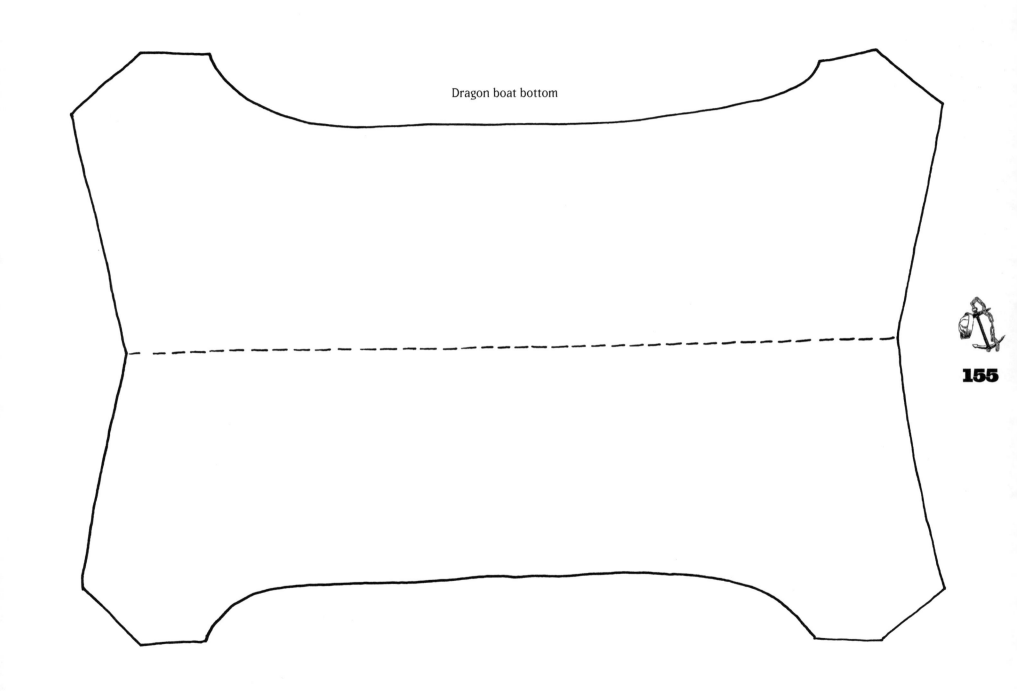

Dragon boat bottom

155

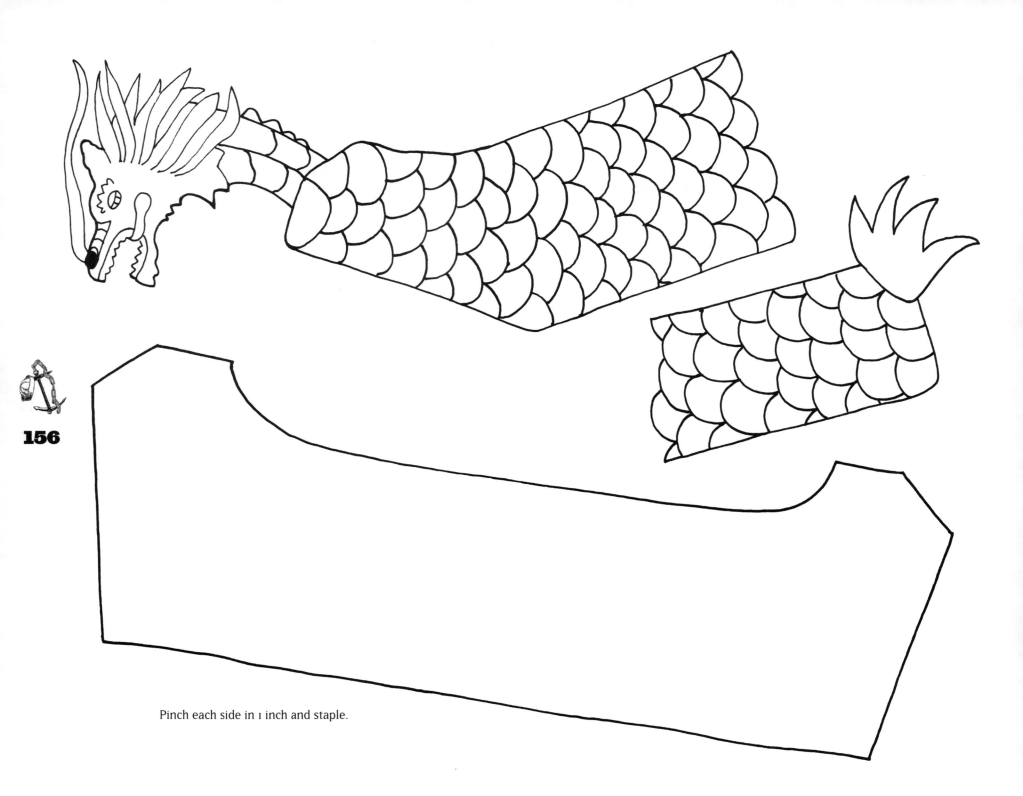

156

Pinch each side in 1 inch and staple.

Bake Bananas

Sailors enjoyed this sweet dessert that the Hawaiians steamed in an underground oven called an imu.

What You Need

2 bananas (firm, with green tips)
Cooking pan
Hot pads
Sugar
Cinnamon

What You Do

1. Preheat the oven to 375°F (190.56°C).
2. Peel the bananas and place them in the pan.
3. Bake for 20 minutes.
4. Using the hot pads, remove (or have an adult help you remove) the pan from the oven.
5. Slice and sprinkle with sugar and cinnamon. Enjoy!

Yield: 2 to 4 servings

String a Flower Garland

Sailors visited hundreds of tiny Pacific islands during the golden age of sail. The natural beauty of the mountains, the people, and the plants must have presented a striking change from the monotony of sea life. The flower garland made of hibiscus, gardenia, and other sweet smelling flowers was a delightful way to enjoy these natural gifts. *Leis*, as they were called, were commonly given to guests as a welcoming gesture. Garlands were also made from shells, ferns, seeds, animal teeth, berries, and seaweed.

What You Need

Heavy-duty white thread, about 35 inches (89 centimeters)

Needle

25 to 30 flower blossoms, fresh or silk

6 clear drinking straws, cut into 1-inch (2.54-centimeter) lengths

Scissors

What You Do

1. Knot the thread about 3 inches (7.62 centimeters) from the end, then thread the needle.
2. Choose one blossom at a time and thread the needle through the middle and out through the stem. After each blossom, pull the thread through a straw piece to separate.
3. Continue with each flower and straw, leaving about 3 inches (7.62 centimeters) on either end of the thread to tie together.

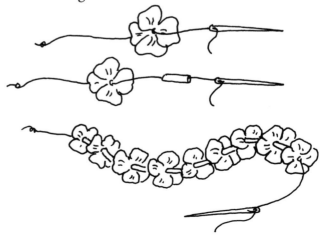

Play No'a: A Hawaiian Game

Hawaiians were warm and welcoming to the sailors. They shared their unique Pacific lifestyle while embracing Western ideas of religion and culture. This is a game that adults and children played together. You need at least four people and no more than 10 to play the game.

What You Need

Several players
Small towel or cloth for every two people playing
A stone

What You Do

1. Divide into two evenly numbered teams. (It's all right if one team has an extra person.)
2. The members of each team sit side by side in a row, with the two rows facing each other. (If you have an extra player, then two people sitting next to each other on one team will be across from just one person on the opposite team.) The opposing players should sit about 3 feet (.91 meters) apart.
3. Put a cloth on the ground between each opposing pair.
4. The team hiding the stone huddles together and picks one member to hide the stone under his or her cloth. Then they sit back down in their original places. To confuse the opposing team, several players pretend to put a stone under their cloths.
5. The guessing team must look very carefully for clues as to where the stone is. Watch people's eyes and body movements. If you think you know which cloth the stone is under, yell out that person's name. If you're wrong, then the other team scores a point; if you're right, your team scores a point.
6. Take turns hiding the stone until one team has scored 10 points.

Play Kimo: Picking Up Stones

Children who had been at sea for months on whaling ships were eager to join in games with Hawaiian children. This is another game from old Hawaii. *Kimo* means "to bob." Players bob their heads up and down while playing. This game is similar to jacks.

What You Need

50 small pebbles or shells

What You Do

1. Two players face each other with the pile of pebbles between them.
2. Pick an unusual stone, one that has a different color or shape, to be your kimo stone.
3. Using only one hand, throw your kimo stone in the air. Pick up another stone with that same hand and catch the kimo stone before it hits the ground. You must use the same hand throughout the game.
4. When you miss, it becomes your opponent's turn. Continue taking turns until all of the pebbles have been picked up. The player who picks up the most stones wins.

Design a Feather Cape

Feathers were a valuable commodity in Hawaii. They were worn as a symbol of power and rank. Chiefs wore feather capes, leis, and helmets as ceremonial garments and in battle. Feathers of yellow and red, the favored colors of royalty, were plucked from the rare i'iwi bird. Feathers were even used to pay taxes. It is estimated that a full-length cape, such as one worn by a king, would take 800,000 feathers from 80,000 birds. The people gathered feathers during molting season (when the birds shed feathers naturally), but they also hunted the birds for their feathers.

Make this festive cape, modeled after one given to Captain Valentine Starbuck of the whaler *L'Aigle* in 1824 by the secretary to Hawaii's King Kamehameha II. He must have been considered an honored guest.

What You Need

Thick layer of newspaper
Brown grocery bag
Scissors
Pencil
Plastic spoon
All-purpose glue
Red, yellow, and black feathers (available in craft stores)
Hole punch
2 12-inch (30.48-centimeter) lengths of ribbon

What You Do

1. Put a layer of newspaper over your work area.
2. Cut out the flattened bottom of the grocery bag by punching a hole in it with the scissors and then cutting along folds.

3. Cut a vertical line in the rest of the bag so that it lies flat in one piece.
4. Fold the bag in half the long way. Keeping the fold on the left, cut a curved line along the right side.
5. Cut a quarter circle into the top left of the folded side for the neck.
6. Open the cape and lay it out flat.
7. With your pencil lightly draw alternating blocks where red, yellow, and black feathers will go. Create your own design.
8. Spread glue over each block using a plastic spoon. Glue on the feathers.
9. Punch a hole in the top of each side of the neck hole.
10. Pull the ribbon through and knot gently. To wear, slip the neck hole over your head with the opening to the cape in the front.

162

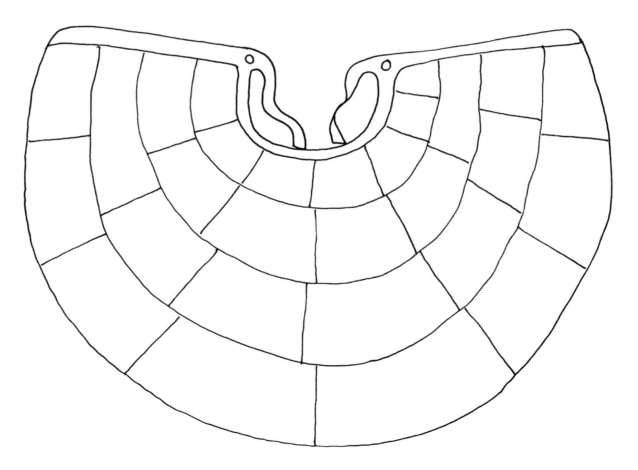

Make a Sailor's Valentine

Artisans in the West Indies made shell mosaics to sell to sailors. These became so popular that they became known as *sailor's valentines*. The original sailor's valentines were octagonal or round wooden boxes that opened with a hinge in the middle, and both top and bottom were decorated.

What You Need

Small heavy cardboard or papier-mâché box (available in craft stores) in a round, octagonal, or heart shape

A few lengths of yarn

100 or more small shells in different shapes and colors (find these on the beach or in a craft store)

All-purpose glue

What You Do

1. Choose either the top or bottom of the box. You will be making the valentine inside it.
2. Glue a heart shape made of yarn in the middle. Glue three concentric circles of yarn around the heart.
3. Sort the shells into piles.
4. Starting from the inside and working out to the edges, glue the shells down. Use the same type shell for each section. Vary the design by gluing some upside down and others right side up.
5. Let dry overnight.

Sailing Alone Around the World: The Voyage of Joshua Slocum

On June 27, 1898, Canadian-born Joshua Slocum sailed into Newport, Rhode Island, to become the first man to singlehandedly sail around the world. It took the 54-year-old Nova Scotian three years and 46,000 miles to accomplish the feat. He withstood stormy, turbulent seas, pirates, ragged coastlines, dangerous currents, and native savages, sometimes sailing for 70 days at a stretch without seeing another human being. He navigated with only the most basic instruments—sextant, compass, charts, lead on a line to measure depth, and a windup clock.

The amazing journey began when Slocum completely rebuilt a run-down skeleton of an oyster sloop named the *Spray*. It took 13 months to restore, and when it was done, the 35-foot sailboat was as seaworthy as any of the clipper ships Slocum had commanded in his distinguished career. Captain Joshua Slocum had already circumnavigated the world many times over.

Slocum wrote a colorful memoir of the voyage entitled *Sailing Alone Around the World*. The book continues to be in print after 100 years, and has been translated into many languages. On November 14, 1909, 65-year-old Captain Slocum set out on what would be his final voyage. He sailed out of Vineyard Haven in Massachusetts in the *Spray* for the Orinoco River in Venezuela and was never heard from again.

Captain Joshua Slocum has become a folk hero of sorts among modern sailors. Many reproductions of the *Spray* have been built, and solo sailors enjoy the challenge of sailing the same route that he took around the world.

All journeys must end, and, happily for the sailor, the journey's end meant going home. This last chapter brings us to the seaports of America. We enjoy some Yankee home cooking, play games by the seashore, and watch seaport craftsmen at work.

The Sailor's Return.
Library of Congress

5

Homeward Bound

Join us as we welcome the ship home! We'll watch the town come alive when the ship pulls into the harbor. Let's offer a bowl of steaming fish chowder to our returning sailors. Afterward, we'll take a peek at some seaport artisans at work. We'll learn how to furl a sail in the sailmaker's loft, make a barrel with the cooper, and build our own miniature wharf. Then it's time for fun and games! Kids had more chores and responsibilities in those days, but they still found time to play. So join us in skipping a stone or two, and try your hand at a game of old maid, and fox and geese.

Seaport Towns

At the first sign of a sail on the horizon, the children flocked to spread the word. Spotting a homebound ship meant a reward of a coin or two. Townspeople climbed to the tops of their homes and hilltops to catch a glimpse of the returning ship.

Soon the docks filled with friends, family, and townspeople. Anyone scrambled down to the harbor went to see if a whaler had *greasy luck* (had filled its hold with whale oil), or to see the exotic goods a ship returning from the Orient might bring. The sailors onboard approached the harbor with a mixture of excitement and dread, happy to be home but fearing they might be greeted with bad news.

Workers scurried to unload the cargo, and boardinghouses and taverns prepared for the sailors' arrival. Hundreds of businesses offered ropes, sails, barrels, rigging, spars, and anchors. Shipyards, counting houses, banks, wood carvers, chandlers, and restaurants—all depended on the business of the sea.

Soon sailors of all races and nationalities adorned with earrings and tattoos roamed the streets. Horse-drawn wagons clopped back and forth from the wharves into town piled high with cargo. Peddlers hawked food, clothing, rooms, and entertainment to the newly paid sailors.

Families were reunited, sweethearts were greeted, and the town was ignited with excitement. The smell

166

Orange Jelly

Jellies (gelatin desserts, like Jell-O) were considered very elegant desserts and were served on special occasions such as a ship's homecoming or on holidays. Eating an orange or drinking a glass of orange juice was considered a great luxury. Most children received one orange a year in their Christmas stockings.

of home-cooked meals wafted on the ocean air, children played with their fathers, and music from homes and taverns filtered through the streets.

During the golden age of sail, seaports were the center of life and commerce in America. From New Bedford, Massachusetts, to Charleston, South Carolina, magnificent tall rigged ships with clouds of white sail filled the sparkling blue harbors. Wharves were lined with slippery casks of whale oil and crates of Chinese porcelain, tea, and silk. There were also high sea tales to share.

Cook New England Fish Chowder

Chowder parties were popular among sea-going families. These were picnic-like celebrations that whaling and merchant families enjoyed while in port and at home. To cook the chowder on the beach they set up a tripod with a hanging kettle and built a fire underneath. Men, women, and children all joined in to help with the cooking. Sometimes there was a chowder master in the group directing who would chop the vegetables or skin the fish. When they were done, the chowder would gently simmer all afternoon as the families went sailing or horseback riding or enjoyed relaxed conversation. The children went swimming, climbed on the rocks, and dug for clams. Chowder parties usually included other food as well—bread, meat, cakes, watermelon, lemonade, and perhaps a pint or two of whiskey.

Here's a recipe so you can organize your own chowder party.

What You Need

A grown-up to assist
4 thick bacon slices
Large pot (nonstick preferred)
Large mixing spoon
Paper towels
3 large potatoes
Potato peeler
Small paring knife
Cutting board
1 large onion
2 pounds (.91 kilograms) haddock or cod

2 teaspoons salt (10 milliliters)
½ teaspoon freshly ground black pepper (2.5 grams)
2 tablespoons flour (17 grams)
½ cup cold water (118 milliliters)
Small bowl
Fork
3 cups (710 milliliters) milk
Chowder crackers (optional)

What You Do

1. Make sure you have adult supervision! Fry the bacon in the pot over medium-high heat until crisp. Stir with the mixing spoon.
2. Remove the bacon to the paper towels, leaving the drippings in the pan.
3. Peel the potatoes and dice into small cubes with the paring knife.
4. Remove the skin from the onion and, using the cutting board, chop it into small pieces.
5. Cook the onion in the bacon drippings over medium-low heat for five minutes.
6. Cut each fish piece in half and put it in the pot. (The fish will break into smaller pieces during cooking.)
7. Break up the bacon and add it back into the pot along with the potatoes and enough water just to cover the food.
8. Add salt and pepper.
9. Bring to a boil over medium-high heat and then lower the heat to simmer the chowder for 30 minutes, stirring frequently.
10. Using a fork, mix the flour and water together in a small bowl. Add the flour mixture to the pot to help the chowder thicken.
11. Now add the milk and cook for 15 minutes longer, or until the potatoes are tender. Serve with chowder crackers if desired.

Yield 8 servings.

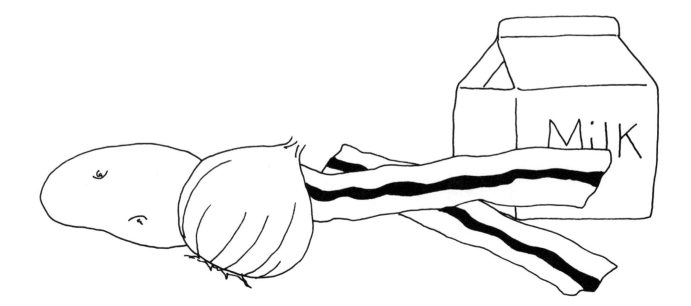

Furl a Sail

The sailmaker's loft was a busy place. Ships returning home nearly always needed to have sails repaired or new sails made. Clouds of white sail puffed from the floors while sailmakers and their apprentices measured, cut, and sewed. The sturdy cloth that moved a multiton clipper ship thousands of miles around the world looked deceptively delicate.

Sailmaking was a painstaking process. The sailmaker first had to measure the masts and yards of the ship. From these measurements he created enormous paper patterns that he laid out on the floor of the loft. Next he cut out the canvas and stitched it together by hand (or in later years by machine). Finally the rope and special fittings were stitched to attach the sail to the ship.

What You Need

3 50-inch (1.27-meter) lengths of nylon "plastic canvas" yarn or any sturdy yarn

3 medium-size safety pins

Scissors

Standard-size white pillowcase

Sturdy coat hanger

What You Do

1. Tie a length of yarn to the small circular part of each safety pin.
2. Fold the pillowcase in half over the bar of the hanger.
3. Pin the double thickness together at the left, right, and middle of the bottom with the safety pins.
4. Pull the yarn loosely over the pillowcase and let it hang over the other side.
5. To see what it was like to furl a sail, pull down on the three lines at the same time.

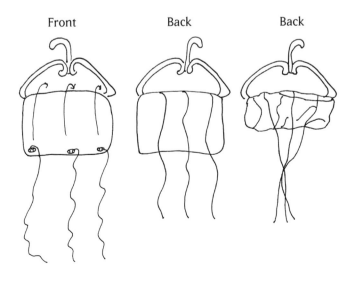

Front   Back   Back

Build a Wharf

Life in American seaport towns centered on the wharves at the harbor, where townspeople could see a bobbing flurry of white canvas furled on enormous masts. Sea wharves were made up of boat docks that faced a number of businesses that outfitted and supplied provisions for ships. Ironworkers toiled over red-hot fires to mold and shape the metal of chains, anchors, and casks. Riggers went aloft in *bosun's chairs* (special chairs made of rope and wood that looked like swings), installing ropes, chains, tackle, and blocks on ships. Everything was geared to the needs of a ship, and the wharf was the ship's home.

What You Need

A grown-up to assist
Layer of newspaper
4 24-ounce (.71-liter) empty
    soda bottles with caps
Sand, pebbles, or pennies
    for weight
Scissors or knife

2 wood paint stirrers (avail-
    able wherever paint is sold)
20 to 25 craft sticks
All-purpose glue
Toy boat (optional)
String (optional)

What You Do

1. Lay a newspaper over your workspace.
2. Fill the bottles halfway with sand, pebbles, or pennies to weigh them down.
3. Have an adult help you to cut a slit long enough for the paint stirrer to slide in about 2 inches (5.08 centimeters) from the top of each of the four bottles.
4. Slide opposite ends of the paint stirrers into the soda bottles so that what you have looks like two long sides of a bridge.
5. Connect the two long sides by gluing craft sticks between them. (It's easier if you pull the stirrers out and do the gluing flat on the newspaper, and then reconnect them to the bottles when the glue has dried. Note: allow several hours for the glue to dry.)
6. To set up your dock, find a gentle stream or pond. Wedge the soda bottles into the sand or mud along the water's edge.
7. Dock your boat at the wharf with string. Now sit back and imagine a fantastic sea voyage.

New Bedford Harbor. *Library of Congress*

Skipping Stones

Kids in seaport towns often snuck in a few minutes to play while doing chores or running errands. A fun activity for children living near the ocean was skipping stones. It cost nothing, the materials were readily available, and they could play for a minute or an hour. Try your hand at skipping stones.

Make a Barrel

Barrels were made in three stages. First, wooden boards were cut into strips and sanded. Then they were fit into wood or metal hoops made by another craftsman known as a hooper. The last step was measuring and cutting the heads (the top and bottom) and assembling the barrel.

Real barrels are made with strips of wood called staves, which are thicker in the middle than at the ends. They bend, which allows them to bulge out in the middle. (In this activity we are going to make a simple barrel with straight staves that do not bend.) Big wooden barrels filled with salt pork, hardtack, flour, water, and other provisions filled the holds of whaling ships. As a two- or three-year voyage wore on, the provisions were consumed and the empty barrels filled with whale oil.

The craftsman who made these barrels was called the *cooper*. His work was highly valued onboard ship.

Extra barrels were made ashore in his cooperage and broken down to save room aboard ship. As the need arose, the cooper put the barrels back together.

What You Need

Layer of newspaper

Round cardboard container with cover (a 1-pint [.47-liter] ice cream container works well)

Brown acrylic paint

Paintbrush

All-purpose glue

Craft sticks

2 rubber bands

Scissors

2 brown cardboard strips about ½ inch by 12 inches (1.27 by 30.48 centimeters)

What You Do

1. Lay newspaper over your work space.
2. Paint the container and the cover the same natural color as the craft sticks. The cover may need two coats.
3. Glue the craft sticks all around the container. It is easier if you put two rubber bands over the container and slip the craft sticks underneath. There will be some gaps, but the paint underneath will make the background blend in.

4. When the glue has dried, remove the rubber bands. Place the cover back on.
5. Cut and glue the brown cardboard strips about 1 inch (2.54 centimeters) from the top and bottom. Now you have a shipboard cask to hold your own treasures!

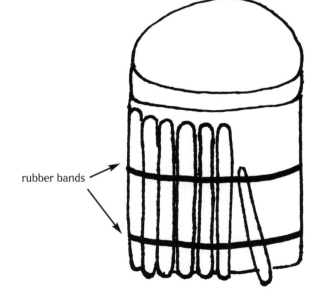

rubber bands

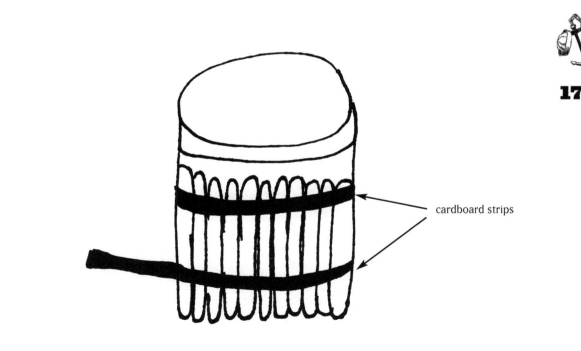

cardboard strips

173

Play Fox and Geese

Fox and geese was an easy game to play onboard a ship or at home. A gameboard could be drawn on paper, whalebone, or wood, or in the sand with a stick. Seamen used whatever was available for game pieces: coins, shells, buttons, and even spare ship's nails.

What You Need

11-by-14-inch (27.94-by-35.56 centimeter) piece poster board or heavy paper
Ruler
Black marker
Game pieces: 13 pennies, buttons, or cardboard circles (These will be the game pieces, or geese.)
1 nickel or thimble (This will be the fox.)

What You Do

1. With a marker and ruler trace the game board on the next page. Do not trace the fox and geese; they show how to set up the game.
2. Match your game pieces to the spaces shown on the board.

How to Play

One person is the fox and the other person is all of the geese. For the geese to win they must completely corner the fox. The fox wins if he can capture enough geese (nine or more) to make it impossible for him to be cornered (all but four or fewer).

Rules for the Fox

The Fox

- Can move one space at a time along any line
- Can move horizontally (side to side), vertically (up and down), or diagonally (along the slanted lines)
- Can capture a goose by jumping over him to an empty spot directly on the other side, as in checkers. He can catch more than one goose in the same move if he can jump to an empty spot after each one. The fox then keeps the captured geese (off the board)

Rules for the Geese

A Goose

- Can move one space along a line, but never backward
- Can move horizontally, vertically (up but not down), and diagonally (forward but not backward)
- Cannot make jumps or capture the fox

The fox always begins. Then the fox and the geese alternate turns. The geese win if they corner the fox, making the fox unable to move. The fox wins when there are four or fewer geese left.

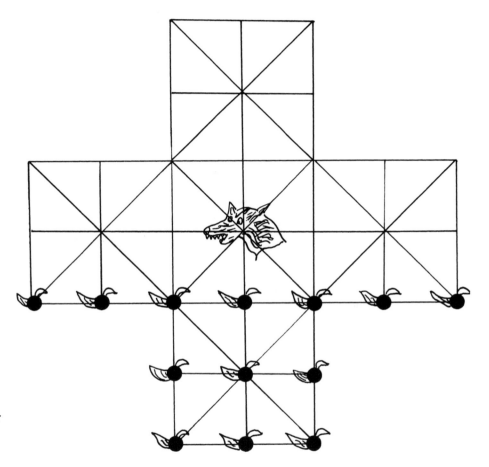

175

Bake Boston Baked Beans

Nothing is more "Olde New England" than Boston baked beans, a staple of every Yankee table. To the sailor the aroma of beans cooking was the smell of home.

What You Need

A grown-up to assist
1 onion, peeled
Cutting board
Small paring knife
Large mixing bowl
2 cans of beans with pork
1 tablespoon (15 grams) brown sugar
¼ cup (60 milliliters) ketchup
1 teaspoon (5 grams) mustard
Mixing spoon
2-quart (1.89-liter) ovenproof baking dish
4 bacon slices

What You Do

1. Preheat the oven to 375°F (190.56°C).
2. Have an adult help you to dice the onion.
3. Mix together all the ingredients except the bacon in the large bowl.
4. Place the mixture in the ovenproof dish. Place bacon pieces over the top.
5. Bake for one hour.

Yield: 6 servings

Boston Baked Beans is also the name of an old-fashioned candy that you can still buy today. The candies are not really beans but candy-coated peanuts.

Pretend with a Ropewalk Game

An old sailor's saying is, "By his ropes ye shall know the measure of the sailor." Rope was the main tool and lifeline of the sailor. Rope pulled in the mighty sails, heaved the ship's enormous anchor, lifted the sailors into the rigging, and whisked them in their whaleboats across the sea attached to the harpooned whale.

In the golden age of sail, thousands of miles of rope were made in the long *ropewalks* of seaport towns. Plant fibers, usually hemp, and in later years manila, were used. The fibers were spun into strands of yarn, and then the rope maker would walk backward, twisting the yarn into rope.

This is a game that children played in seaport towns. The players mimic the actions of the rope maker.

What You Need

Four or more players   Measuring tape
Chalk   4 or more players

What You Do

1. Divide into two teams of at least two people each.
2. With the chalk draw two 30-foot (9.14 meters) parallel lines about 5 feet (1.52 meters) apart. Two ropewalkers line up at the beginning of each line. The others on the team work as apprentices, assisting the ropewalker by calling out to him to move to the left or right.
3. The game begins when an assigned person yells, "Ready, set, go!" The ropewalkers then walk backward to the end of the line and turn around and walk back. They must keep at least one foot on the line at all times or they get sent back to the starting line.
4. The first team to have all its ropewalkers finish wins.

177

Hemp is an herb that grows out of the ground. The fiber extracted from the stem of the plant has been used for hundreds of years in making rope, paper, and many other products.

Play Dominoes

Playing dominoes was a popular way for children and sailors alike to pass the time at sea and at home. They made dominoes from ivory, whalebone, and wood.

What You Need

2 pieces, 9 by 12 inches (22.86 by 30.48 centimeters), of 2-millimeter-thick self-stick foam sheets, any light color (available in craft stores)

1 piece, 9 by 12 inches (22.86 by 30.48 centimeters), 2-millimeters-thick (non-self-stick foam sheet, any light color; available in craft stores)

Pencil

Ruler

Black marker

Scissors

What You Do

1. Stack the three sheets of foam on top of one another using the sticky sides to attach to the nonstick sides. Press down well to adhere.

2. Draw a grid of 1-inch-by-1-inch (2.54-by-2.54-centimeters) blocks with the pencil. Each domino will be a double block, and together they will represent every possible toss of two dice plus blank blocks. There will be 28 double blocks in all.

3. Follow the diagram and color in the dots with the marker. Press down to make indentations.

4. Draw a line with the marker across the middle of each double block.

5. Cut the double blocks out along the lines with scissors.

Here's the pattern they should follow.

(Blank–blank) (Blank–1) (Blank–2) (Blank–3) (Blank–4) (Blank–5) (Blank–6)

(1–1) (1–2) (1–3) (1–4) (1–5) (1–6)

(2–2) (2–3) (2–4) (2–5) (2–6)

(3–3) (3–4) (3–5) (3–6)

(4–4) (4–5) (4–6)

(5–5) (5–6)

(6–6)

How to Play (2–4 players)

Place the dominoes face down between the players. Each player chooses seven dominoes (choose five if you have three or four players). To view your "hand" without the other players seeing it, place the dominoes on their sides. The player with the highest pips (number of dots) on a single domino goes first. That player must show it to prove that he has the highest number of dots, then, place down the domino (in this case a 6, 5). The next player must lay down a domino where one side has the same number of dots as one side of the first domino. So the second player decides to put down a 5, 3 (the sides showing the 5 dots are touching). Now the next player must match the open end of one of the dominoes, either the 6 or the 3. If a player does not have a domino to match, then she must pick from the pile of remaining dominoes. If a doublet (domino where both sides have the same number of dots) is used, it is placed crossways to the domino it is matching. The first player to get rid of all his or her dominoes wins.

Make a Figurehead

Highly skilled American craftsmen carved the magnificent wooden sculptures that adorned the bows of sailing ships. Although the art of chiseling figureheads is ancient, the independent and patriotic American spirit allowed these craftsmen to break free of European ideas of artistry and design and create their own unique folk art. In addition, American figurehead carvers took full advantage of the abundant pine available in the New World.

Ship-carving shops were always located close to shipyards. An American carver learned his trade by working an average of five years as an apprentice in a shop before he could strike out on his own. Ship builders and architects had close contact with the carvers. When they came into a carver's shop they made chalk sketches of the particular ship's bow so that the carver knew how the figurehead should be placed. Ideas and sketches were discussed until a design was decided on. Popular figures on American ships were eagles, American Indians, famous people, lions, women, and gods and goddesses.

Figureheads were carved as full figures, half figures, or busts. Frequently the figure had one foot extended, which gave the illusion of movement. In the early years, carvers painted figureheads that were lavish in their use of color. In the clipper ship years, figureheads were painted white with touches of gold and sometimes bronze.

If you were lucky enough to be a rich shipbuilder during the golden age of sail, you could commission the carver to make any kind of figurehead you wanted. Shipbuilders often had their own or one of their children's image used as a figurehead. Sometimes they would instead use a symbol representing the ship's name. What would you choose as your personal symbol? A pair of skates? A guitar? Your dog?

What You Need

4–8 ounces (113 to 227 grams) of lightweight air-dry
   modeling compound*
Paint or colored markers (optional)

What You Do

1. Mold your figurehead into the desired shape.
2. Mold a scroll to provide the base for your figurehead.
3. Press the figurehead into the scroll, allowing the figure to lean forward a bit, as it would on a ship. If it
   is a person, have one foot stepping forward.
4. Let dry overnight. (It will still be a bit spongy.)
5. Paint or color with markers if desired.

Ships' figureheads in East India Hall. *Peabody Essex Museum*

181

*Note: The amount of compound you use depends on how large a figurehead you will
be making. Approximately 4 to 6 inches (10.16 to 15.24 centimeters) high works best.
You can choose to buy either a multipack of different colors of compound or a package
of white compound, which you can color with acrylic paint or markers.

Drop Jack Straws

(2–4 players)

Children in seaport towns played games such as jack straws, which is very similar to pick-up sticks. In old New England, this game was played with real straw. Here's an easy game you can create using wooden barbeque skewers.

What You Need

25 to 30 wooden skewers
5 or 6 felt-tip markers in different colors

What You Do

1. Color the skewers, using a different color for every five sticks. (If you color the sticks, each player selects a color and only picks up these sticks.) To make the game more difficult, leave the sticks unpainted. Now you're ready to play!

2. Hold all the sticks in your hand and then drop them from a height of about 6 inches (15.24 centimeters) from the floor.

3. The first player picks up one stick at a time, being careful not to move any of the other sticks. If a player moves a stick by accident, his or her turn is over.

4. The next player gathers all the sticks to start the drop again. The player who has the most points in three turns wins.

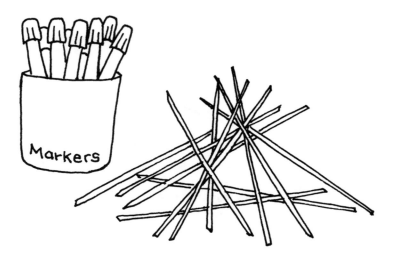

Cook Wampanoag Clam Casserole

The Yankees followed the example of the Native Americans and took advantage of the Atlantic coast's abundant seafood. You can make a version of this hearty New England dish.

What You Need

A grown-up to assist

Mixing spoon

Mixing bowl

50 crumbled buttery crackers

2 six-ounce (170.1-gram) cans of minced clams, including the juices

1 can cream of mushroom soup

2 eggs

1 cup (237 milliliters) milk

½ teaspoon (2.5 milliliters) onion powder

Freshly ground black pepper to taste

2-quart (1.89-liter) casserole dish greased with butter

What You Do

1. Preheat the oven to 350°F (176.67°C).
2. Using a large mixing spoon, mix all the ingredients together in a bowl.
3. Pour the mixture into the baking dish.
4. Bake for one hour uncovered.
5. Allow to cool slightly and serve. Enjoy!

Yield: 6 servings

Play Old Maid

(2 or more players)

Old maid, like many of the games children enjoyed in seaport towns, is still played today. This easy card game was introduced in the mid-1800s and immediately became a children's favorite. It is usually played with a standard deck of cards, but there are also special old maid decks with crazy characters on each card. Try your hand at avoiding the old maid.

What You Need

Deck of playing cards

What You Do

1. Remove one of the queens and set it aside. You will be playing with the other 51 cards.

2. Deal all the cards. Not everyone will have the same number, but it won't matter.

3. Before you start, each player removes all the pairs (two of the same card, but not three or four) from his or her hand. Each player places all the pairs face down on the table.

4. The dealer holds her cards so only she can see them and lets the player to the left pick one.

5. If that card matches another one in his hand, the second player places the pair face down on the table. If it does not make a pair then the player must keep the card in his hand.

6. Now the next player to the left chooses a card from the second player, and so on. The first player to match all his or her cards is the winner. Only one person will be stuck with a queen that can't be matched up. That person loses because he or she couldn't get rid of the old maid.

Although the days of the great sailing ships are over, the history of the lives the sailors led will remain with us forever. We can breathe the salty air and stroll the harbors of the great seaports such as New Bedford, Nantucket, and New York just as they did. We can see the ships they sailed at our maritime museums, read the logs and journals they kept, sing the songs they sang, hear the stories they told, speak the language they spoke, make the crafts they made, and enjoy the seaport communities they left behind.

Conclusion

The seas were the first highways of the world. From the time ancient people tied logs together to make a raft, human beings have used the sea to explore their world. By the end of the 19th century, the era of the sailing ship had passed by. Sail was replaced by steam, and wood was replaced by steel. After a series of technological advances, diesel or gas turbine engines drive most of today's ships.

Today's merchant or cargo ships are far larger than the sailing ships. Without all the work of the sails and rigging, these vessels need much smaller crews to operate them. Passenger or cruise ships are now as comfortable and luxurious as fine hotels, a far cry from the packet ships of the 19th century. They are generally used for leisure travel rather than as a means of transportation.

Modern merchant seamen work on commercial ships or for the *merchant marine* (a fleet of ships that carry cargo during peacetime, but may be used to transport troops and military goods in wartime). Their duties include standing lookout; steering the ship; maintaining deck equipment such as anchors,

The Fate of Whales Today

In recent years, international groups concerned about saving the whales have slowly made progress by passing laws to ban whaling. An organization known as the International Whaling Commission (IWC) was founded in 1946 to limit the number and species of whales that could be hunted. The members of the IWC agreed to a worldwide moratorium (delay or suspension of activity) on whaling, which was put into effect in 1986. The IWC now has 38 member nations. Some are for commercial whaling; some are against it. The organization was designed to give every nation a voice regarding international whaling rules.

Currently, the only nation in the world that hunts whales commercially is Norway. The Norwegians broke with the moratorium in 1993 to hunt the minske whale. Whale hunting also takes place for aboriginal subsistence. This means that aboriginal people, original inhabitants of an area, may hunt whales to use for food, shelter, and clothing. The Alaskan Inuit are aboriginal people who hunt whales for subsistence. Japan practices something called scientific whaling. It is supposed to provide important information about whale populations, but whale protection organizations believe it is just commercial whaling in disguise because part of the practice involves selling whale meat at a profit.

life jackets, and boats; and operating cargo-moving equipment in port. They also participate in the ship's maintenance and upkeep. Although working conditions have improved immensely, sailors are still away for long periods of time. They have to work through storms and bad weather, and suffer all the risks of working at sea. Unlike the old days, however, most newer vessels serve good food and have clean, comfortable living conditions.

Today sailing is mostly a leisure activity. Many people own their own small sailing boats. One of the few opportunities left to see a full-size operating sailing ship is at a tall ships celebration or event. On these occasions great sailing ships (some historical reproductions, some new) from all over the world meet to race, cruise, and travel to a series of ports where the public can visit. If a tall ships exhibition comes to a seaport near you, take advantage of the opportunity to climb aboard. Walk the ship's decks, climb into its fo'c'sle, steer at the wheel, peek into the galley, run your hands along the capstan, and crane your neck to see a sky filled with masts, sails, and rigging. Then close your eyes and imagine that you are in the age of sailors and whalers—and you're off on a fantastic sea voyage.

Resources

Glossary

aft: Toward the stern or back of the ship.

aloft: Above the deck, in the rigging.

ambergris: A substance found in the intestines of sperm whales, used in the manufacture of perfume.

astern: Behind the ship.

baleen: Cartilage found in the jaws of whales.

baleen whales: Whales that have rows of soft cartilage instead of teeth. They use this cartilage as a strainer to feed on small marine creatures called krill.

ballast: Weight in the hold of the ship that helps to keep the vessel stable.

belaying pin: A wooden pin used to secure lines.

blockade runners: Ships that are able to slip though a naval blockade in order to deliver war materials, food, and supplies.

blubber: Whale fat.

boatheader (lancer): The officer who steered the boat and lanced the whale.

boatsteerer (harpooner): The officer who harpooned the whale then steered the whaleboat.

boatswain (bosun): The officer in charge of deck maintenance and crew.

bosun's chair: A special chair made of rope and wood that carried the rigger aloft.

bowsprit: A large spar that projects forward from the stern of a ship.

cabin: Living quarters onboard a ship.

capstan: A mechanical device used to pull up the anchor.

case: The top of the sperm whale's head, which holds spermaceti.

cask: A barrel-like container used on a whaler.

cat-o'-nine-tails: A knotted leather rope used to flog sailors who misbehaved or broke rules.

catwalk: A narrow shipboard passageway.

chandler: A merchant who specializes in selling goods used aboard ship.

chanteyman: A singer who leads sailors in a sea chantey.

clipper ship: A sailing ship designed for speed with a sharp bow, narrow hull, and large expanse of sails.

cooper: A barrel maker.

cordage: The rope or line aboard ship.

crimp: A person who tricked sailors into signing up for the crew of another ship.

crow's nest: The platform for the lookout at the top of the mast.

cutting in: Removing the blubber and bone from the whale.

dandyfunk: Sailor's treat made of hardtack and molasses.

deck: Permanent covering over a compartment or hull of the ship, which serves as a floor.

ditty box: A small box a sailor used for sewing supplies and personal items.

dogwatch: The two short shifts of the day, 4:00 to 6:00 P.M., and 6:00 to 8:00 P.M., designed so that no one was on watch for the same hours every day.

drogue: A wooden block used to slow a whale after being harpooned.

figurehead: A wooden sculpture on the bow of a sailing ship.

fore or forward: Near the bow or front of the vessel.

forecastle (fo'c'sle): Group living quarters of the sailors, below decks in the front of the ship.

Fresnel lens: An important invention for lighthouses that allows light rays to focus into a single strong beam that can be seen for miles.

galley: The ship's kitchen.

gam: A social event that took place when ships anchored together at sea.

gasket: Short pieces of rope that secure a sail to a yard.

greasy luck: When a ship returned home with its holds filled with whale oil.

greenhand: A sailor on his first voyage.

grub: Sailor's food.

guano: Bird droppings that were harvested and used for fertilizer.

guernsey: Tight-fitting wool shirt worn by sailors.

gurry: A mix of blood, seawater, and oil—a byproduct of the trying-out processing of whales.

halyard: Line for hoisting yards and sails.

hardtack: A hard cracker made with salt and flour.

harpoon: The instrument used to fasten the whaleboat to a whale. It has a barbed iron head and a long wooden shaft.

hen frigate: A ship on which the captain's wife and family accompanied the crew.

hogshead: A container of liquid, a barrel.

hold: Space below decks of a ship, used for storage.

hornpipe: a type of dance common to seafarers; also a tin flute.

hull: The frame or main body of the ship.

idler: A crew member who specializes in one skill.

Jack Tar: Slang for a sailor, who typically had tar on his clothes.

jib: The foremost sail of a ship.

jib-boom: A long pole that extends under the jib.

jib topsail: A main sail located above the jib.

junk: The lower half of the forehead of the whale, which holds sperm oil.

keel: The centerline of the boat running fore and aft. A timber that the frame of the ship is built on.

kid: A wooden tub with iron hoops that held the sailors dinner.

lance: The sharp weapon used to kill the whale after it is harpooned.

land shark: A person who makes a living by overcharging sailors for goods and services.

larboard: Old name for the left side of a vessel when facing forward. The more current term is *port*.

lay: A whaleman's share of the earnings of his voyage.

liberty: Free time during which sailors are allowed to leave the ship.

lobscouse: Salt beef and hardtack stew. It sometimes included vegetables.

lubber: A clumsy sailor.

marlinspike sailor: A sailor who is a master at tying knots.

masthead: The top of a mast.

mate: The first officer in rank after the captain of the ship.

mating: A situation in which two ships hunted the same whale and split the profits.

merchant marine: Fleet of ships that carry cargo in peacetime but may be used to transport troops and war materials during wartime.

merchant ship: A ship used to haul goods.

Middle Passage: Part of the triangular route of the Atlantic slave trade, when the slaves were brought from Africa to the New World.

Morse code: A code consisting of dots and dashes that represent letters and can be tapped out with a special device to communicate from ship to ship.

oilskin: Canvas soaked in oil or tar.

old salt: An experienced sailor.

packet ships: A fleet of ships that carried passengers, mail, and cargo on a regular schedule.

plum duff: Flour pudding, sometimes made with raisins.

port: Left side of a vessel when facing forward.

privateers: Private ships that were granted permission from the government to take over enemy ships in wartime.

ropewalk: A long building where ropes are made.

running rigging: Lines that adjust a ship's sails.

salt horse: Salt beef.

salt junk: Salt pork.

scrimshaw: Designs carved into whalebone and whales' teeth.

scupper: A drain on the deck of a ship.

sea chantey: Sailor's work song.

sea chest: A wooden chest that held a sailor's personal belongings.

sextant: A tool used in navigation.

shoot the sun: To measure the altitude of the sun with a sextant.

slop chest: The ship's store, which sold goods to the sailors at high prices.

soger: A sailor who pretended to be sick to avoid work.

sound: To dive deep.

spar: A strong pole onboard ship such as a boom, mast, or yard.

spermaceti: A white, waxy substance obtained from the head of the sperm whale. Used to make smokeless candles.

standing rigging: Fixed lines that secure a ship's yards and masts.

starboard: The right side of the ship when facing forward.

stay: Large ropes used to support masts.

steerage: The between-decks quarters for passengers on packet ships.

stern: The back portion of a ship.

steward: A sailor who serves meals and does housekeeping in the cabin.

stove: Smashed a hole in.

supercargo: An officer in charge of selling and trading a ship's cargo.

toothed whale: A type of whale that has two or more teeth and feeds on a variety of fish.

trying-out: The job of boiling whale blubber into oil.

trypots: Cooking vessels used to boil blubber into oil.

tryworks: The brick stove where the blubber was boiled out.

whaleboat: The small, narrow boat that was used to hunt the whale.

whaleman: A member of a whaling crew.

whaler: A whaling ship.

yarn: A sailor's story.

190

Bibliography

Books for Children

Abernethy, Jane Fulton, and Suelyn Ching Tune. *Made in Hawaii.* Honolulu, HI: University of Hawaii Press, 1983.

Carrick, Carol. *Whaling Days.* New York: Clarion Books, 1993.

Carse, Robert. *The Young Mariners: A History of Maritime Salem.* New York: Norton, 1966.

Chase, Mary Ellen. *Donald McKay and the Clipper Ships.* Boston: Houghton Mifflin, 1959.

Coggins, Jack. *Flashes and Flags: the Story of Signaling.* New York: Dodd Mead, 1963.

Cosgrave, John O'Hara. *Clipper Ship: America's Famous and Fast-Sailing Queens of the Sea.* New York: Macmillan, 1963.

Dana, Richard Henry. *Two Years before the Mast: A Personal Narrative of Life at Sea.* Garden City, NY: Nelson Doubleday, 1949.

De Pauw, Linda Grant. *Seafaring Women.* Boston: Houghton Mifflin, 1982.

Duncan, Fred B. *Deepwater Family.* New York: Pantheon Books, 1969.

Gemming, Elizabeth. *Blow Ye Winds Westerly: The Seaports and Sailing Ships of Old New England.* New York: Crowell, 1971.

Giambarba, Paul. *Whales, Whaling, and Whalecraft.* Centerville: Scrimshaw Publishing, 1967.

Goldsmith-Carter, George. *Sailing Ships and Sailing Craft.* New York: Grosset and Dunlap, 1970.

Gourley, Catherine. *Hunting Neptune's Giants: True Stories of American Whaling.* Brookfield, CT: Millbrook Press, 1995.

Humble, Richard. *Timelines: Ships, Sailors, and the Sea.* New York: Franklin Watts, 1991.

Jernegan, Laura. *A Whaling Captain's Daughter: The Diary of Laura Jernegan, 1868–1871,* ed. Megan O'Hara. Mankato, MN: Blue Earth Books, 2000.

Jones, Dorothy Holder, and Ruth Sexton Sargent. *Abbie Burgess, Lighthouse Heroine.* Camden, ME: Down East Publishing, 1969.

Kalman, Bobbie. *Arctic Whales and Whaling.* Toronto, CN: Crabtree, 1993.

Loeper, John J. *The Shop on High Street: The Toys and Games of Early America.* New York: Atheneum, 1978.

Lyon, Jane D. *Clipper Ships and Captains.* New York: American Heritage Publishing Co., 1962.

MacFarlan, Alan and Paulette. *Knotcraft.* New York: Bonanza Books, 1967.

McCague, James. *When Clipper Ships Ruled the Seas.* Champaign, IL: Garrard Publishing, 1968.

McGowen, Tom. *Album of Whales.* New York: Checkerboard Press, 1980.

Meadowcroft, Enid LaMonte. *When Nantucket Men Went Whaling.* Champaign: Garrard Publishing, 1966.

Murphy, Jim. *Gone-a-Whaling: The Lure of the Sea and the Hunt for the Great Whale.* New York: Clarion Books, 1998.

Myers, Walter Dean. *Amistad: A Long Road to Freedom.* New York: Dutton Children's Books, 1998.

Plude, Catherine. "Honolulu: Nineteenth-Century Yankee Seaport." *Cobblestone.* April 1988, pp. 22–25.

Purdy, Susan Gold. *Eskimos.* New York: Watts, 1982.

Readers Digest Association. *American Folklore and Legend.* Pleasantville, NY: Readers Digest Association, 1978.

Roop, Peter. *Keep the Lights Burning, Abbie.* Minneapolis: First Avenue Editions, 1985.

Roop, Peter, and Connie Roop. *Good-bye for Today: The Diary of a Young Girl at Sea.* New York: Atheneum Books, 2000.

Ross, Stewart. *Fact or Fiction: Pirates.* Brookfield, CT: Copper Beech Books, 1995.

Shapiro, Irwin. *The Story of Yankee Whaling.* New York: American Heritage Publishing Co., 1960.

Stein, R. Conrad. *The Story of the New England Whalers.* Chicago: Children's Press, 1982.

Stonehouse, Bernard. *A Visual Introduction to Whales, Dolphins, and Porpoises.* New York: Checkmark Books, 1998.

Tamarin, Alfred H. *Voyaging to Cathay: Americans in the China Trade.* New York: Viking Press, 1976.

Van Note, Peter. *Tangrams: Picture-Making Puzzle Game.* Rutland, VT: C. E. Tuttle, 1966.

The Visual Dictionary of Ships and Sailing. New York: DK Publishing, 1991.

Wade, Mary Dodson. "Who Got the Money?" *Cobblestone.* April 1984, pp. 13–14.

Wilkinson, Phillip. *Ships.* New York: Kingfisher, 2000.

Books for Adults

Albion, Robert G., William A. Baker, and Benjamin W. Labaree. *New England and the Sea.* Mystic, CT: Mystic Seaport Museum, 1972, 1994.

Allen, Everett S. *Children of the Light: The Rise and Fall of New Bedford Whaling and the Death of the Arctic Fleet.* Boston: Little Brown, 1973.

Altimiras, J. *Sailing Knots.* New York: Arco Publishing, 1984.

Ashley, Clifford W. *The Ashley Book of Knots.* Garden City, NY: Doubleday and Company, 1944.

Barstow, Robbins. *Meet the Great Ones: An Introduction to Whales and Other Cetaceans.* Wethersfield, CT: Cetacean Society International, 1987.

Beavis, Bill, and Richard G. McCloskey. *Salty Dog Talk: The Nautical Origins of Everyday Expressions.* London: Adlard Coles Nautical, 1983.

Bockstoce, John R. *Whales, Ice, and Men: The History of Whaling in the Western Arctic.* Seattle: University of Washington Press in association with the New Bedford (MA) Whaling Museum, 1986.

Botting, Douglas S. *The Pirates.* Alexandria, VA: Time-Life Books, 1978.

Carlisle, Rodney P., and J. Welles Henderson. *Marine Art and Antiques: Jack Tar, a Sailor's Life 1750–1910.* Woodbridge, Suffolk: Antique Collectors Club, 1999.

Carpenter, Francis Ross. *The Old China Trade: Americans in Canton, 1784–1843.* New York: Coward, McCann and Geoghegan, 1976.

Church, Albert Cook. *Whale Ships and Whaling*. New York: W. W. Norton and Co., 1938.

Cloud, Enoch Carter. *Enoch's Voyage: Life on a Whaleship*. Wakefield, RI: Moyer Bell, 1994.

Cogill, Burgess. *When God Was an Atheist Sailor: Memories of a Childhood at Sea 1902–1910*. New York: Norton, 1990.

Creighton, Margaret S. "The Captains' Children: Life in the Adult World of Whaling, 1852–1907." *American Neptune Magazine*, July 1988, pages 203–216.

———. *Dogwatch and Liberty Days: Seafaring Life in the Nineteenth Century*. Worcester: The Peabody Museum, 1982.

———. *Rites and Passages: The Experience of American Whaling 1830–1870*. New York: Cambridge University Press, 1995.

Cutler, Carl C. *Greyhounds of the Sea: The Story of the American Clipper Ship*. Annapolis, MD: Naval Institute Press, 1984.

Druett, Joan. *Hen Frigates: Wives of Merchant Captains Under Sail*. New York: Simon and Schuster, 1998.

———. *Petticoat Whalers: Whaling Wives at Sea 1820–1920*. Auckland, AU: Collins, 1991.

Dudden, Arthur Power. *The American Pacific: From the Old China Trade to the Present*. New York: Oxford University Press, 1992.

Durant, John, and Alice Durant. *Pictorial History of American Ships*. New York: A. S. Barnes and Co., 1953.

Ellis, Richard. *Men and Whales*. New York: Knopf, 1991.

Ely, Ben-Ezra Stiles. "There She Blows": A Narrative of a Whaling Voyage, in the Indian and South Atlantic Oceans*. Middletown, CT: Published for the Marine Historical Association by Wesleyan University Press, 1971.

Freehand, Julianna. *A Seafaring Legacy: the Photographs, Diaries, Letters, and Memorabilia of a Maine Sea Captain and His Wife, 1859–1908*. Camden, ME: Picton Press, 1994.

Frere-Cook, Gervis. *The Decorative Arts of the Mariner*. Boston: Little Brown, 1966.

Garner, Stanton, ed. *The Captain's Best Mate: The Journal of Mary Chipman Lawrence on the Whaler Addison, 1856–1860*. Hanover, NH: University Press of New England, 1966.

Harlow, Frederick Pease. *The Making of a Sailor, or Life Aboard a Yankee Square Rigger*. New York: Dover Publications, 1988.

Hawes, Dorothy Schurman. *To the Farthest Gulf: The Story of the American China Trade*. Ipswich: Ipswich Press, 1990.

Heckman, Richard D. *Yankees Under Sail: A Collection of the Best Sea Stories from Yankee Magazine, with Rare Photographs Taken during the Age of Sail*. Dublin, NH: Yankee Publishing, 1968.

Hegarty, Reginald B. *Birth of a Whaleship*. New Bedford: New Bedford Public Library, 1964.

Hendrickson, Robert. *Salty Words*. New York: Hearst Marine Books, 1984.

Hilton, Joseph C. *Letters to His Son: Boyhood Under Sail: 1874–1881*. *American Neptune Magazine*.

Hinz, Earl R. *The Complete Book of Anchoring and Mooring*. Centerville, MD: Cornell Maritime Press, 1994.

Hulbert, Anne. *Victorian Crafts Revived*. New York: Hastings House, 1978.

Kromer, Helen. *Amistad—The Slave Uprising aboard the Spanish Schooner*. Cleveland: The Pilgrim Press, 1997.

Labaree, Benjamin Woods. *America and the Sea: A Maritime History*. Mystic, CT: Mystic Seaport Publishing, 1998.

Laing, Alexander. *Seafaring America*. New York: American Heritage Publishing, 1974.

Linsley, Leslie. *Scrimshaw: A Traditional Folk Art, A Contemporary Craft*. New York: Hawthorn Books, 1976.

Maddocks, Melvin. *The Atlantic Crossing (The Seafarers)*. Alexandria, VA: Time-Life Books, 1981.

Maloney, Elbert, S. *Chapman Piloting, Seamanship, and Small Boat Handling*. New York: Heart Marine Books, 1999.

Mawer, G. Allen. *Ahab's Trade: The Saga of South Sea Whaling*. New York: St. Martin's Press, 1999.

McKay, Richard C. *Some Famous Sailing Ships and Their Builder Donald McKay*. Riverside, CT: Seven C's Press, 1928, 1969.

McLure-Mudge, Jean. *Chinese Export Porcelain for the American Trade 1785–1835*. Newark, DE: University of Delaware Press, 1962.

Melville, Herman. *Moby Dick*. Washington Square Press, New York: 1999.

Miller, Russell. *The East Indiamen*. Alexandria, VA: Time-Life Books, 1980.

Morton, Harry Miller. *The Wind Commands: Sailors and Sailing Ships in the Pacific*. Middletown, CT: Wesleyan Press, 1975.

Ola, Per and Emily D'Aulaire. "Around the World Alone." *Smithsonian Magazine*. 29, no. 2 (1998): 118–134.

Oliver, Sandra Louise. *Saltwater Foodways: New Englanders and Their Food, at Sea and Ashore, in the Nineteenth Century*. Mystic, CT: Mystic Seaport Museum, 1995.

Olmsted, Francis Allyn. *Incidents of a Whaling Voyage*. Rutland, VT: C.E. Tuttle Co., 1969.

Petroski, Catherine. *A Bride's Passage: Susan Hathorn's Year Under Sail*. Boston: Northeastern University Press, 1997.

Philbrick, Nathaniel. *In the Heart of the Sea: The Tragedy of the Whaleship Essex*. New York: Viking Press, 2000.

Pinckney, Pauline A. *American Figureheads and Their Carvers*. Port Washington, NY: Kennikat Press, Inc., 1940.

Raph, Theodore. *The American Song Treasury: 100 Favorites*. New York: Dover Publications, Inc., 1986.

Rogers, John G. *Origins of Sea Terms*. Mystic, CT: Mystic Seaport Museum, Inc., 1985.

Rosenow, Frank. *The Ditty Bag Book*. Boston: Nimrod Press, 1976.

Shay, Frank. *A Sailor's Treasury*. Norton and Co., New York: 1951.

———. *Iron Men and Wooden Ships: Deep Sea Chanties*. Garden City, NJ: Doubleday, 1924.

Smith, Hervey Garrett. *The Marlinspike Sailor*. Tuckahoe, New York: J. DeGraff, 1971.

Snow, Edward Rowe. *New England Sea Tragedies*. New York: Dodd Mead, 1960.

———. *Pirates and Buccaneers of the Atlantic Coast*. Boston: Yankee Publishing Co., 1944.

———. *Women of the Sea*. New York: Dodd Mead, 1962.

Villiers, Captain Alan. *Men, Ships, and the Sea*. Washington, DC: National Geographic Society, 1962.

Whipple, A. B. C. *Yankee Whalers in the South Seas*. Rutland, VT: C.E. Tuttle Co., 1973.

———. *Vintage Nantucket*. Chester, CT: The Globe Pequot Press, 1978.

———. *The Clipper Ships*. Alexandria, VA: Time-Life Books, 1980.

———. *The Whalers*. Alexandria, VA: Time-Life Books, 1979.

Whiting, Emma Mayhew, and Henry Beetle Hough. *Whaling Wives*. Boston: Houghton Mifflin, 1954.

Wier, Albert E. *The Book of a Thousand Songs*. New York: Carl Fischer Inc., 1918.

Wilbur, Keith, C. *Tall Ships of the World: An Illustrated Encyclopedia*. Chester, CT: Globe Pequot Press, 1986.

Willets, William. *Chinese Art*. New York: George Braziler, 1958.

Williams, Harold (editor). *One Whaling Family*. Boston: Houghton Mifflin, 1964.

193

Maritime Museums

United States

California

Los Angeles Maritime Museum
Berth 84, Foot of Sixth Street
San Pedro, CA 90731
(310) 548-7618
E-mail: museum@
    lamaritimemuseum.org
www.lamaritimemuseum.org
The museum features a vast collection of ship and boat models, a display of seamen's knots you can try, and the resident tugboat, *Angels Gate.*

Maritime Museum of Monterey
5 Custom House Plaza
Monterey, CA 93940
(831) 372-2608
www.mntmh.org/maritime.htm
The Fresnel lens from the Point Sur Lighthouse illuminates the museum. Includes exhibits on merchant trading, life onboard ship, the hide and tallow trade of the 19th century, and the sardine industry. Special treasure maps guide young visitors through the museum.

San Diego Maritime Museum
1492 North Harbor Drive
San Diego, CA 92101
(619) 234-9153
E-mail: info@sdmaritime.org
www.sdmaritime.com
San Diego's Maritime Museum is home to one of the most significant historic ship collections in the world, including *The Star of India*, which is said to be the world's oldest active sailing ship.

San Francisco Maritime National
    Historical Park
Building E, Fort Mason Center
San Francisco, CA 94123
(415) 561-7100
E-mail: SAFR_Ranger_Activities
    @nps.gov
www.nps.gov/safr
The park features a fleet of National Historic Landmark vessels, a maritime museum, a maritime library and an urban park/public beach at the north end of Fisherman's Wharf. Rangers present history programs and lead tours.

Connecticut

Mystic Seaport
75 Greenmanville Avenue
P.O. Box 6000
Mystic, CT 06355-0990
(888) 9SEAPORT
E-mail: visitor.services@
    mysticseaport.org
www.mysticseaport.org
Mystic Seaport is the largest and most comprehensive maritime museum in North America. It has a 17-acre (6.88 hectare) waterfront that berths several historic sailing ships, including the *Charles W. Morgan*, the last surviving whaleship. The museum features the re-creation of an 1800s seaport where you can visit the Charles Mallory Sail Loft, the Plymouth Cordage Company, the Ship Carver's Shop, and much more.

U.S. Coast Guard Museum
15 Mohegan Avenue
New London, CT 06320-8511
(860) 444-8511
E-mail: CHerrick@cga.uscg.mil
www.uscg.mil/hq/g-cp/museum/
    museum index.html
The museum displays one of the only first-order Fresnel lenses in the United States. The figurehead from the Coast Guard training ship *Eagle* hangs as if mounted on the bow of a ship, one of the largest figureheads exhibited in the United States.

Hawaii

Hawai'i Maritime Center
Pier 7, Honolulu Harbor
Honolulu, HI 96813
(808) 536-6373
www.bishopmuseum.org/hmc
The exhibits cover the *Falls of Clyde*, a four-masted fully rigged ship built in 1878; King Kalakaua's Boathouse Museum; and Hawaii's past and present relationship to the whale.

Maine

Maine Maritime Museum
243 Washington Street
Bath, ME 04530
(207) 443-1316
E-mail: maritime@bathmaine.com
www.mainemaritimemuseum.org
On the banks of the Kennebec River is the historic Percy & Small shipyard, which constructed the largest ever wooden sailing vessel built in the United States.

Penobscot Marine Museum
Church Street at U.S. Route 1
P.O. Box 498
Searsport, ME 04974-0498
(207) 548-2529
E-mail: museumoffices@
    penobscotmarinemuseum.org
www.penobscotmarinemuseum.org
Seafaring village of eight historic buildings, all still located on one street. The buildings include the Fowler-True-Ross house and barn, a former sea captain's home, and the Nickels-Colcord-Duncan barn, which houses a watercraft collection.

Portland Harbor Museum at Spring
    Point
Southern Maine Technical College
Fort Road
South Portland, ME 04106
(207) 799-6337
E-mail: phm@gwi.net
www.portlandharbormuseum.org
The museum has a permanent exhibition on *Snow Squall*, the last American clipper ship. The Spring Point Ledge Lighthouse is open for public tours three or four times each summer.

Maryland

Calvert Marine Museum
14200 Solomons Island Road
P.O. Box 97
Solomons, MD 20688
(410) 326-2042
E-mail: information@
    calvertmarinemuseum.com
www.calvertmarinemuseum.com
Highlights of the museum include a hands-on discovery room, Chesapeake-built wooden boats, a

woodcarving shop, and the Drum Point Lighthouse and the Cove Point Lighthouse (1828), which is still in operation.

Chesapeake Bay Maritime Museum
Navy Point
Mill Street
P.O. Box 636
St. Michaels, MD 21663-0636
(410) 745-2916
E-mail: letters@cbmm.org
www.cbmm.org
Highlights of the museum include the world's largest collection of traditional bay boats and the fully restored 1879 Hooper Strait Lighthouse. Interactive exhibits display the sport and art of Chesapeake decoys, steamboats, and oystering.

USS *Constellation*
Pier 1
301 East Pratt Street
Baltimore, MD 21202-3134
(410) 539-1797
E-mail: administration@ constellation.org
www.constellation.org
The USS *Constellation* is the last all-sail warship built by the U.S. Navy, and it is open to the public as a museum. The museum features maritime artifacts from the Civil War period.

Maryland Historical Society Radcliffe Maritime Museum
201 West Monument Street
Baltimore, MD 21201
(410) 685-3750
E-mail: museum@mdhs.org
www.mdhs.org/explore/maritime
The museum's maritime collection centers on the history of the Chesapeake Bay and the Port of Baltimore.

U.S. Naval Academy Museum
118 Maryland Avenue
Annapolis, MD 21402
(410) 293-2108
www.usna.edu/Museum
The museum's collections show the Navy's role in war and in peace. The United States Navy Trophy Flag Collection begun in 1814 totals more than 600 historic American and captured foreign flags, including the famous "Don't Give Up the Ship" flag flown at the Battle of Lake Erie.

Massachusetts

Essex Shipbuilding Museum
66 Main Street on Route 133
Essex, MA 01929
(978) 768-7541
E-mail:info@ essexshipbuildingmuseum.org
www.essexshipbuildingmuseum.org
The museum has more than 7,000 shipbuilding artifacts including tools, photographs, ship models, and more. A highlight of the museum, the *Evelina M. Goulart*, is one of seven surviving Essex schooners.

Whaling Museum
Nantucket Historical Association
13 Broad Street
Nantucket, MA 02554
(508) 228-1894 ext. 0
E-mail: nhainfo@nha.org
www.nha.org
Originally built as a spermaceti candle factory, the Whaling Museum now holds a rare collection of whaling artifacts including a 28-foot (8.53-meter) whaleboat, South Seas artifacts, and a collection of scrimshaw. Summer workshops include making faux scrimshaw and sailors' valentines. Special attractions include a retelling of the tragedy of the whaleship *Essex*.

New Bedford Whaling Museum
Old Dartmouth Historical Society
18 Johnny Cake Hill
New Bedford, MA 02740
(508) 997-0046
www.whalingmuseum.org
This is the largest and most comprehensive whaling museum in the world. Collections include a half-scale model of the whaling bark *Lagoda*, hundreds of harpoons and whaling implements, figureheads, scrimshaw, Pacific and Arctic souvenirs from whalemen, four full-sized whaleboats, and the skeleton of a humpback whale.

Peabody Essex Museum
East India Square
Salem, MA 01970-3783
(978) 745-9500
(800) 745-4054
E-mail: pem@pem.org
www.pem.org
The museum's new maritime gallery will feature its expansive collection of paintings, nautical instruments, charts, ship models, figureheads, and oceanic art from the islands.

USS *Constitution* Museum
Charlestown Navy Yard
P.O. Box 1812
Boston, MA 02129
(617) 426-1812
Museum: www.ussconstitutionmuseum.org
Ship: www.ussconstitution.navy.mil
The USS *Constitution*, "Old Ironsides," is the oldest commissioned warship afloat in the world. The museum features hands-on exhibits and historic artifacts.

Michigan

Michigan Maritime Museum
260 Dyckman Avenue (Black River Waterfront)
P.O. Box 534
South Haven, MI 49090
(800) 747-3810
www.michiganmaritimemuseum.org
This museum's attractions include historical watercraft used on Michigan's waterways, ship and boat models, marine motors and engines, maritime art, tools and equipment used in the maritime trades, and everyday life in maritime regions.

New Jersey

Tuckerton Seaport
120 West Main Street, Box 52
Tuckerton, NJ 08087
(609) 296-8868
E-mail: tuckcport@aol.com
www.tuckertonseaport.org
Here you'll find an authentic working seaport village. There are 16 re-created historic structures representing the trades and crafts of the Barnegat Bay region, including Tucker's Island Lighthouse, Joe Dayton's Sawmill, and Parson's Clam and Oyster House.

New York

American Merchant Marine Museum
U.S. Merchant Marine Academy
300 Steamboat Road
Kings Point, NY 11024
(516) 773-5000
www.usmma.edu/museum
The museum houses more than 50 ship models (including an 18-foot [5.49-meter] model of the passenger ship SS *Washington*), one of the best collections of old and rare navigational instruments, and a Japanese surrender sword from World War II.

Cold Spring Harbor Whaling
   Museum
Main Street
P.O. Box 25
Cold Spring Harbor, NY 11724
(516) 367-3418
www.cshwhalingmuseum.org
The museum features a 19th-century
   whaleboat, a scrimshaw collection,
   and a whale conservation exhibit.

East End Seaport Museum and
   Marine Foundation
Third Street at the Ferry Dock
P.O. Box 624
Greenport, NY 11944
Foundation: (631) 477-0004
Museum: (631) 477-2100
E-mail: eseaport@aol.com
www.eastendseaport.org
This museum has several Fresnel
   lenses on display and exhibits on
   the first submarines, fishing, the
   America's Cup Race, and light-
   house restoration.

Erie Canal Museum
318 Erie Boulevard East
Syracuse, NY 13202
(315) 471-0593, ext. 13
E-mail: andy@eriecanalmuseum.org
www.eriecanalmuseum.org
The museum has 40,000 photographs depicting the Erie and
   Barge Canals between 1850 and
   the present. Attractions include a
   full-size replica of an Erie Canal
   line boat and a penny postcard
   arcade.

Hudson River Maritime Museum
50 Rondout Landing
Kingston, NY 12401
(845) 338-0071
E-mail: hrmm@ulster.net
www.hrmm.org
This museum features exhibits on
   the maritime history of the
   Hudson River: steamboats, tug-

boats, ferries, and the ice-cutting
   and brick-making industries. The
   highlight of the museum is the
   Rondout Lighthouse, a working
   lighthouse that was built in 1915.
   This is accessible only by regularly scheduled boat trips at the
   museum.

Long Island Maritime Museum
86 West Avenue
P.O. Box 184
West Sayville, NY 11796
(631) HISTORY
E-mail: limaritimemuseum@aol.com
www.limaritime.org
This museum features exhibits of
   Long Island shipwrecks, oystering
   on Long Island, and a boat-build-
   ing school. *Priscilla* is the museum's recently restored 1888 oyster
   sloop.

South Street Seaport Museum
207 Front Street
New York, NY 10038
(212) 748-8610
www.southstseaport.org
The museum houses the nation's
   largest fleet of privately maintained historic vessels, including
   some moored for visitation and
   others designated as training ships.
   A new core exhibition, *World Port
   New York*, will explore the history
   of the port in seven buildings and
   24 new galleries.

North Carolina

Graveyard of the Atlantic Museum
59158 Coast Guard Road
Hatteras, NC 27943
(252) 986-2995
E-mail: museum@
   graveyardoftheatlantic.com
www.graveyardoftheatlantic.com
This is a unique museum dedicated
   to shipwrecks along the coast of
   North Carolina. Exhibits include

shipwrecks related to exploration,
   transportation, commerce, and
   piracy, as well as exhibits about
   the discovery and preservation of
   shipwrecks.

North Carolina Maritime Museum
315 Front Street
Beaufort, NC 28516
(252) 728-7317
E-mail: maritime@ncmail.net
www.ah.dcr.state.nc.us/sections/
   maritime/default.htm
The North Carolina Maritime
   Museum seeks to preserve and
   interpret the state's rich maritime
   heritage through educational
   exhibits, programs, and field trips.
   The museum conducts a sailing program for children eight and older.

Ohio

Great Lakes Historical Society
   Inland Seas Maritime Museum
408 Main Street
P.O. Box 435
Vermilion, OH 44089
(800) 893-1485
E-mail: glhs1@inlandseas.org
www.inlandseas.org
Exhibits include Great Lakes shipwrecks, lighthouses, and the pilot-
   house from the ship, *Canopus*.

Oregon

Columbia River Maritime Museum
1792 Marine Drive
Astoria, OR 97103
(503) 325-2323
E-mail: abney@crmm.org
www.crmm.org
This museum features the maritime
   history of the Pacific Northwest.
   Interactive exhibits invite you to
   pilot a tugboat, participate in a
   Coast Guard rescue, walk on the
   bridge of a World War II Navy
   destroyer, and explore the light-
   ship *Columbia*.

Pennsylvania

Erie Maritime Museum/U.S. Brig
   Niagara
150 East Front Street
Erie, Pennsylvania 16507
(814) 453-2744
E-mail: sail@brigniagara.org
www.brigniagara.org
The Erie Maritime Museum is home
   to the U.S. Brig *Niagara*, the
   reconstructed flagship of
   Commodore Oliver Hazard Perry
   in the Battle of Lake Erie, one of
   the most important United States
   victories in the War of 1812. An
   interesting exhibit is a reconstruc-
   tion of a portion of the U.S. Brig
   Lawrence, which was fired upon
   by the *Niagara*.

Independence Seaport Museum
Penn's Landing Waterfront
211 S. Columbus Boulevard at
   Walnut
Philadelphia, PA 19106-1415
(215) 925-5439
E-mail: seaport@indsm.org
www.phillyseaport.org
Visitors to the Independence Seaport
   Museum can climb aboard the
   oldest floating steel warship in the
   world, the cruiser *Olympia*, which
   fought in the Spanish-American
   War. And tour the World War II
   submarine *Becuna*.

Texas

Texas Seaport Museum
Pier 21, #8
Galveston, TX 77550
(409) 763-1877
E-mail: Elissa@galvestonhistory.org
www.tsm-elissa.org
Home of the *Elissa*, a 125-year-old
   fully restored sailing barque that
   sails   several times a year. The
   maritime museum contains a scale
   model of the Galveston seaport in
   the 1800s.

Vermont

Lake Champlain Maritime
  Museum
Basin Harbor Road
Rural Route 3, Box 4092
Vergennes, VT 05491
(802) 475-2022
E-mail: info@lcmm.org
www.lcmm.org
A dozen exhibit buildings feature
  aspects of Lake Champlain history: boat building (including
  live demonstrations),
  Revolutionary War exhibits, a
  blacksmith shop, 200 preserved
  collections from shipwrecks, and
  a horse ferry.

Virginia

Hampton Roads Naval Museum
One Waterside Drive
Norfolk, VA 23510-1607
(757) 322-2987
E-mail:
  gbcalhoun@nsn.cmar.navy.mil
www.hrnm.navy.mil
The museum features an 1850 U.S.
  Navy seaman round coat and
  several ship models and prints.
  Highlights are items from the
  war sloop USS *Cumberland* and
  the Confederate raider CSS
  Florida.

The Mariner's Museum
100 Museum Drive
Newport News, VA 23606
(757) 596-2222
E-mail: info@mariner.org
www.mariner.org
This is one of the largest and most
  comprehensive maritime museums in the world. Visitors can
  interact with gallery interpreters
  and see actual artifacts from the
  sunken Civil War ironclad USS
  Monitor—its revolving gun tur-
  ret, engine, condenser, and more.

Portsmouth Naval Shipyard Museum
2 High Street
Portsmouth, VA 23704
(207) 438-3975
www.ports.navy.mil/museum.html
The museum exhibits include half-
  hull models of 19th-century ships
  built at the shipyard, scale models,
  pieces from the Naval Prison and
  the Spanish-American War, and
  German U-boats.

The Old Coast Guard Station
24th Street & Oceanfront
P.O. Box 24
Virginia Beach, VA 23458
(757) 428-1587
E-mail: ocgsedu@macs.net
www.oldcoastguardstation.com
The museum is housed in a 1903 former U.S. life-saving station. It is
  filled with rescue equipment used
  by turn-of-the-century surf men to
  save shipwrecked crews.

Washington

Center for Wooden Boats
1010 Valley Street
Seattle, WA 98109-4468
(206) 382-2628
E-mail: cwb@cwb.org
www.cwb.org
There are more than 100 wooden
  boats here, which you are invited to
  explore, rent, or learn to sail. You
  can also build your own boat in the
  center's classes. There are rowboats,
  sailboats, paddleboats, and more.

Northwest Seaport
1002 Valley Street
Seattle, WA 98109
(206) 447-9800
www.nwseaport.org
Highlights of the museum include the
  schooner *Wawona*, the 1889 tugboat *Arthur Foss*, the 1904 light-
  ship *Swiftsure,* and monthly sea-
  chantey programs.

Puget Sound Maritime Historical
  Society
P.O. Box 9731
Seattle, WA 98109
(206) 624-3028
E-mail: president@pugetmaritime.org
www.pugetmaritime.org
The museum centers on the maritime
  history of the Pacific Northwest.

Washington, D.C.

National Museum of American
  History
Smithsonian Institution
14th and Constitution Avenue, N.W.
Washington, DC 20560
(202) 357-2025
  (Transportation/Maritime Line)
E-mail: webmaster@
  americanhistory.si.edu
www.americanhistory.si.edu
The National Watercraft Collection
  includes original artifacts, ship
  models, arts and crafts, ship design
  plans, and the shipwreck of the
  Continental gunboat *Philadelphia*.

Wisconsin

Wisconsin Maritime Museum
75 Maritime Drive
Manitowoc, WI 54220
(920) 684-0218
www.wimaritimemuseum.org
In the museum you can walk through
  the re-creation of a Great Lakes
  port, see how ships were built,
  watch maritime movies, and visit a
  model ship gallery.

Canada

British Columbia

Maritime Museum of British
  Columbia
28 Bastion Square
Victoria, BC V8W 1H9
(250) 385-4222
E-mail: programs@mmbc.bc.ca
www.mmbc.bc.ca

Special features of this museum include
  Tilikum, a dugout canoe used by
  Captain John Voss, who set out to
  circumnavigate the world in 1901.
  Theme galleries explore such topics
  as Captain Cook, Canadian Pacific
  Steamships, and the Royal Navy.

Vancouver Maritime Museum
1905 Ogden Avenue (in Vanier Park)
Vancouver, BC V6J 1A3
(604) 257-8300
E-mail: genvmm@vmm.bc.ca
www.vmm.bc.ca
Highlights of this museum are the
  Alcan Children's Maritime Discovery
  Centre, the famous Canadian
  schooner *St. Roch*, pirates, shipwrecks, and more.

Nova Scotia

Maritime Museum of the Atlantic
1675 Lower Water Street
Halifax, NS B3J 1S3
(902) 424-7490
E-mail: lunnge@gov.ns.ca
www.maritime.museum.gov.ns.ca
This museum houses one of the largest
  collections of maritime artifacts in
  Canada. Exhibits include the sinking
  of the RMS *Titanic*, the Halifax
  explosion of 1917, Nova Scotia's
  golden age of sail, the age of steam,
  indigenous small craft, and Nova
  Scotia's naval heritage.

Ontario

Marine Museum of the Great Lakes at
  Kingston
55 Ontario Street
Kingston, ON K7L 2Y2
(613) 542-2261
E-mail: marmus@marmuseum.ca
www.marmus.ca
This museum features an internationally recognized collection of Great
  Lakes memorabilia and an extensive
  library with archives for young students and scholars.

Historic Lighthouses

Lighthouses are owned by a variety of groups and people, including the U.S. and Canadian coast guards, national parks, cities and towns, museums, historical societies, and private citizens. Many lighthouses have been converted to serve new functions. There are lighthouses that are homes, inns, restaurants, youth hostels, stores, and tourist centers. One is even a post office.

As modern technology has progressed, lighthouses have become less important as navigational aids. Lighthouses that are no longer needed often fall into disrepair and run the risk of being destroyed. Civic-minded groups and individuals are working to preserve these wonderful structures. The United States has responded by starting the National Historic Lighthouse Preservation Program. This program turns over ownership of lighthouses free of charge to groups that agree to maintain them and keep them open to the public.

Lighthouses do not always have telephone numbers or Web sites. Always find out as much information as you can about a lighthouse before traveling to one, as they can be in remote or difficult-to-reach locations.

For additional information on specific lighthouses in the United States, visit the Maritime Heritage Program on the National Park Service Web site: www.cr.nps.gov/maritime/ltaccess.html. You might also try the Lighthouse Explorer Database at the Lighthouse Depot Web site at: www.lighthousedepot.com (for the United States, Canada, and elsewhere).

Some of these Web addresses have capital letters. Be sure to type them in as capital letters.

United States

California

North Coast

Battery Point (Crescent City) Light
(707) 464-3089
www.northerncalifornia.net/
recreation/batterypoint/
batteryschedule.html

Point Arena Light
(707) 882-2777
www.mcn.org/1/palight

Point Cabrillo Light
(707) 937-0816
www.pointcabrillo.org

Central Coast

Point Pinos Light
(831) 648-5716
www.pgmuseum.org

Point Sur Light
(831) 667-0528
www.lighthouse-pointsur-ca.org

San Francisco Bay Area

Oakland Harbor Light
(510) 536-2050
www.quinnslighthouse.com

Point Bonita Light
(415) 556-0560
www.nps.gov/goga/mahe/pobo

Point Reyes Light
(415) 669-1534

San Diego County

Old Point Loma Light
(619) 557-5450
www.nps.gov/cabr/lighthouse.html

Connecticut

Sheffield Island (Norwalk) Light
(203) 838-9444
www.seaport.org/mainpages/sheffield.
html

Stonington Harbor Light
(860) 535-1440
www.stoningtonhistsoc.org/light.htm

Delaware

Fenwick Island Light
(410) 250-1098 (summer)
(302) 436-8410 (winter)

Florida

Gulf Coast

Gasparilla Island (Boca Grande) Light
(941) 964-0060 or (941) 964-0375
www.dep.state.fl.us/parks/district4/
gasparillaisland/index.asp

South Atlantic Coast

Cape Florida Light
(305) 361-5811
www.dep.state.fl.us/parks/district5/
billbaggscape/index.asp

Jupiter Inlet Light
(561) 747-6639

Key West Light
(305) 294-0012
www.kwahs.com/lighthouse.htm

Ponce de Leon (Mosquito) Inlet Light
(386) 761-1821
www.ponceinlet.org

St. Augustine Light
(904) 829-0745
www.staugustinelighthouse.com

Georgia

Sapelo Island Light
(912) 485-2251

St. Simons Island Light
(912) 638-4666
www.saintsimonslighthouse.org/
direct.htm

Tybee Island Light
(912) 786-5801
www.tybeelighthouse.org

Illinois

Grosse Point Light
(847) 864-5181
www.laddarboretum.org/light.htm

Indiana

Michigan City Light
(219) 872-6133
www.michigancity.com/MCHistorical/
index.html

Maine

Marshall Point Light
(207) 372-6450
www.mainemuseums.org/htm/
museumde tail.php3?orgID=57

Portland Head Light
(207) 799-2661
www.portlandheadlight.com

Seguin Island Light
(207) 443-4808
www.seguinisland.org

Shore Village Museum
104 Limerock Street
Rockland, ME 04841
(207) 594-0311

Spring Point Ledge Light
(207) 799-6337
www.portlandharbormuseum.org

Maryland

Concord Point (Havre de Grace)
Light
(410) 939-9040
www.havredegracemd.com/
VisitorsCenter/PointsOfInterest/
Default.htm

Drum Point Light
(410) 326-2042
www.calvertmarinemuseum.com/
drum_point.htm

Seven Foot Knoll Light
(410) 396-3453
www.natlhistoricseaport.org/
seven.html

Massachusetts

Boston Harbor Light
(781) 740-4290
www.fbhi.org

Cape Cod Highland Light
(508) 487-1121
www.trurohistorical.org/lighthouse.htm

Cape Poge Light
(508) 627-3599
www.trustees.vineyard.net/Tours.htm

Nauset Light
(508) 240-2612
www.nausetlight.org

Ned's Point Light
E-mail: nedspointlight@attbi.com

Scituate Light
(781) 745-1083
www.scituatehistoricalsociety.org/
sites_lighthouse.html

Three Sisters Lights (Three Towers)
(508) 255-3421
www.cr.nps.gov/maritime/park/
threesis.htm

Michigan

Lake Superior

Au Sable Light
(906) 387-3700
www.cr.nps.gov/maritime/park/
ausable.htm

Big Bay Point Light
(906) 345-9957
www.lighthousebandb.com

Crisp Point Light
(906) 492-3206
www.geocities.com/crisppointlths

Copper Harbor Light
(906) 289-4215
www.sos.state.mi.us/history/museum/
musewil/chlight.html

Eagle Harbor Light
(906) 289-4990
www.keweenawhistory.org/eh.html

Point Iroquois Light
(906) 437-5272

Rock Harbor Light
(906) 482-0984
www.cr.nps.gov/maritime/park/
rockhbr.htm

Sand Hills Light
(906) 337-1744
www.sandhillslighthouseinn.com

Whitefish Point Light
(877) SHIPWRECK
www.shipwreckmuseum.com/
museumindex.html

Lake Michigan

Big Sable Point (Grand Point Au
Sable) Light
(231) 845-7343
www.bigsablelighthouse.org

Grand Traverse Light
(231) 386-7195
www.grandtraverselighthouse.com

Sand Point (Escanaba) Light
(906) 786-3763

Seul Choix Point Light
(906) 283-3183
www.reiters.net/lighthouse/
history.html

South Manitou Island Light
(231) 326-5134
www.cr.nps.gov/maritime/parks/
smanitou.htm

White River Light Station
(231) 894-8265
www.whiteriverlightstation.org

Lake Huron

Fort Gratiot Light
(810) 982-3659
www.phmuseum.org/lighthouse.htm

Pointe Aux Barques Light
(989) 328-4749
www.huroncountyparks.com/
lighthouse.htm

Presque Isle Lights
(989) 595-9917

Sturgeon Point Light
www.midwestconnection.com/
lighthouses/lk_huronLT/
SturgeonPointLT.htm

Minnesota

Split Rock Light
(218) 226-6372
www.mnhs.org/places/sites/srl

Two Harbors Light
(218) 834-4898
www.lighthousebb.org/restoration

New Jersey

North

Navesink Twin Lights
(732) 872-1814
www.highlandsnj.com/history/html/
twinlights.html

Sandy Hook Light
(732) 872-5970
www.njlhs.burlco.org/sandyhk.htm
Sea Girt Light
(732) 974-0514
www.lonekeep.com/seagirtlighthouse

South

Absecon Light
(609) 449-1360
www.abseconlighthouse.org

Barnegat Light
(609) 494-2016
www.state.nj.us/dep/forestry/parks/
barnlig.htm

Cape May Point Light
(609) 884-5404
www.capemaymac.org/Lighthouse/
lighthouse-main.htm

Finns Point Rear Range Light
www.gorp.com/gorp/resource/us_nwr/
nj_supaw.htm

Hereford Inlet Light
(609) 522-4520
www.herefordlighthouse.org

Tinicum Island Rear Range Light
www.njlhs.burlco.org/trrlhs.htm

New York

Lake Erie

Dunkirk (Point Gratiot) Light
(716) 366-5050
www.netsync.net/users/skipper/
index.html

Lake Ontario

Fort Niagara Light
(716) 745-7611
www.cr.nps.gov/maritime/light/
fortniag.htm

Port of Genesee (Charlotte-Genesee)
Light
(716) 621-6179
www.frontiernet.net/~mikemay

Sodus Point Light
(315) 483-4936
www.peachey.com/soduslight

Thirty Mile Point Light
(716) 795-3885

Tibbetts Point Light
(315) 654-3450
www.community.syracuse.com/cc/
tibbettspointhostel

East

Fire Island Light
(631) 661-4876
www.fireislandlighthouse.com

Horton Point Light
(631) 765-5500
www.longislandlighthouses.com/
hortonpoint

Jeffrey's Hook Light
(212) 304-2365
www.lighthousemuseum.org/nylights/
lred.html

Montauk Point Light
(888) MTK-POINT (outside of 631
area code)
(631) 668-2544 (Ext. 22 or 23)
www.montauklighthouse.com

Rondout Creek (Kingston) Light
(914) 338-0071
www.ulster.net/~hrmm/rondout/
light.htm

Saugerties Light
(914) 247-0656
www.saugertieslighthouse.com

Stony Point Light
(914) 786-2521
www2.lhric.org/spbattle/spbattle.htm

North Carolina

Bald Head "Old Baldy" Light
(910) 457-5000
www.oldbaldy.org

Bodie Island Light
(252) 473-2111
www.nps.gov/caha/bdlh.htm

Cape Lookout Light
(252) 728-2250
www.nps.gov/calo/lths.htm

Currituck Beach Light
(252) 453-4939
www.currituckbeachlight.com

Ohio

Ashtabula Harbor Light
(440) 964-6847
www.knownet.net/users/Coblentz/
ashmus.html

Grand River (Fairport Harbor) Light
(440) 354-4825

Marblehead Light (Sandusky Bay
Light)
(419) 797-4530
www.dnr.state.oh.us/parks/parks/
marblehead.htm

Oregon

Cape Blanco Light
(541) 332-0248
www.or.blm.gov/coosbay/recreation/
blanco.htm

Cape Meares Light
(800) 551-6949
www.capemeareslighthouse.org

Coquille River (Bandon) Light
(541) 347-2209
www.bandonworld.com/thelight

Heceta Head Light
(541) 547-3696
www.HecetaLighthouse.com

Umpqua River Light
(541) 271-4631

Yaquina Bay Light
(541) 265-5679
www.yaquinalights.org/ybay.html

Yaquina Head Light
(541) 574-3100
www.yaquinalights.org/index.htm

Rhode Island

Beavertail Light
(401) 423-3270
www.beavertaillight.org
Block Island (North) Light
(401) 364-9124

Block Island (Southeast) Light
(401) 466-5009
Rose Island Light
(401) 847-4242
www.roseislandlighthouse.org

Texas

Point Isabel (Port Isabel) Light
(800) 276-6102

Vermont

Colchester Reef Light
(802) 985-3346
www.shelburnemuseum.org/htm/
museum/buildings_collections/
buildings/lighthouse/light.htm

Virginia

Cape Henry Light
(757) 422-9421
www.apva.org/apva/light.html

Washington

Admiralty Head Light
(360) 679-7391
www.cr.nps.gov/maritime/light/
admiralty.htm

Grays Harbor (Westport) Light
(360) 268-0078
www.westportwa.com/museum

Mukilteo Light
(425) 355-4141
www.cr.nps.gov/maritime/light/
mukilteo.htm

North Head Light
(360) 642-3078
www.cr.nps.gov/maritime/light/
northhd.htm

Wisconsin

Lake Michigan

Cana Island Light
(920) 743-5958
www.dcmm.org/canaisland.html

Eagle Bluff Light
(920) 743-5958
www.dcmm.org/eagle.html

Port Washington Light Station
(262) 284-7240
www.portlightstation.org

Lake Superior

Devils Island Light
(715) 779-3398
www.nps.gov/apis/devils.htm

Michigan Island Lights
(715) 779-3398
www.cr.nps.gov/maritime/park/
michisl.htm

Raspberry Island Light
(715) 779-3398
www.nps.gov/apis/raspberr.htm

Sand Island Light
(715) 779-3398
www.nps.gov/apis/sand.htm

Canada

British Columbia

Fisgard Light
(250) 478-5849
www.fisgardlighthouse.com

Pilot Bay Light
www.fogwhistle.ca/bclights/pilot/

New Brunswick

Cape Enrage Light
www.capenrage.org/beta/
lighthouse.html

Fredericton Light
Managed by the city of Fredericton.
The lighthouse is at the bottom of
Regent Street in Fredericton.

Green's Point Light
www.freewebz.com/greenspoint

Swallowtail Light
www.swallowtailinn.com

Newfoundland

Cape Bonavista Light
(709) 468-7444
www.bonavista.net/attractions/
lighthouse.html

202

Cape Pine Light
www.geocities.com/nf_lighthouse
_society/capepine.html

Cape Ray Light
www.lorneslights.com/NF/nf134.html

Cape Spear Light
(709) 772-5367
www.lorneslights.com/NF/nf101.html

Cow Head Light
(709) 243-2446

Fort Amherst Light
www.lorneslights.com/NF/nf104.html

Point Amour Light
www.labradorstraits.net/ptamour.shtml

Quirpon Light
www.linkumtours.com/f_inn.htm

Rose Blanche Light
www.geocities.com/rblighthouse

Nova Scotia

Annapolis Royal Light
Managed by Canadian Coast Guard.
Take Route 108 into Annapolis
Royal and the lighthouse will be
on your left at St. George Street.

Burntcoat Head Lighthouse Replica
(902) 758-2299
www.ednet.ns.ca/educ/heritage/nslps/
burntcoat.htm#Island

Cape D'Or Light
www.ednet.ns.ca/educ/heritage/nslps/
cap_dor.htm

Five Islands Light
Five Island Lighthouse Preservation
Society
P.O. Box 60
Five Islands, Nova Scotia B0M 1K0

Forchu Head Light
(902) 742-1433
www.ednet.ns.ca/educ/heritage/nslps/
cape_forchu.htm

Fort Point Lighthouse
(902) 354-5260
www.ednet.ns.ca/educ/heritage/nslps/
fort_point.htm

Gilberts Cove Light
(902) 837-5584
www.ednet.ns.ca/educ/heritage/nslps/
gilberts_cove.htm

Hampton Light
(902) 665-2138
www.ednet.ns.ca/educ/heritage/nslps/
Hampton.htm

Henry Island Light
(902) 787-2515
www.members.aol.com/w1bkr

Mabou Harbour Light
(902) 945-2982
E-mail: ducharme@ctp.auracom.com

Peggy's Point Light
www.ednet.ns.ca/educ/heritage/nslps/
peggys1.htm
Seasonal post office. Peggy is the
name of the ghost that haunts this
lighthouse. The legend says that
she died in a shipwreck and was
washed ashore on the rocks here.

Port Bickerton Light
(902) 364-2000
www.ednet.ns.ca/educ/heritage/nslps/
pt_bickerton.htm

Port Greville Light
(902) 348-2060
www.ednet.ns.ca/educ/heritage/nslps/
pt_greville.htm

Seal Island Light
(902) 637-2185
www.bmhs.ednet.ns.ca/cshs/sil.htm

Walton Light
Minas Basin, Route 215
Walton, Nova Scotia B0N 2R0

Ontario

Cabot Head Light
(519) 795-7780
www.naturalretreat.com/lighthouses/
cabothead.htm

False Duck Light
www.pec.on.ca/mariners-museum

McKay Island Light
(705) 785-3473 (summer)
(705) 942-0416 (winter)
www.brucebaycottages.com/
Lighthouse.htm

Mississagi Lighthouse Heritage Park
and Campground
(705) 282-7258
(705) 283-1084

Point Clark Light
(519) 571-5684
www.continuouswave.com/misc/
pointClark.html

Port Burwell Light
(519) 874-4807
www.pt-burwell-lighthouse.ca

Presqu'ile Point Light
(613) 475-4324
www.rudyalicelighthouse.net/OntLts/
Prsqle/Prsqle.htm

Windmill Point Light
(623) 925-2896

Prince Edward Island

Cape Bear Light
(902) 962-2917

East Point Light
(902) 357-2106
www.gov.pe.ca/infopei/
onelisting.php3?number=598

Leards Range Rear Light
(902) 357-2106
www.gov.pe.ca/infopei/
onelisting.php3?number=41625

Panmure Head Light
(902) 838-3568
www.gov.pe.ca/infopei/
onelisting.php3?number=610

West Point Light
(902) 859-3605
www.peisland.com/westpoint/light.htm

Wood Islands Light
(902) 962-3110

Quebec

Cap de la Madeleine Light
Managed by: Association Touristique
de Rivière-la-Madeleine. Take
highway 132 (in Rivière-la-
Madeleine) to the Rue du Phare.

Cap-des-Rosiers Light
www.gaspe-forillon.com/english/
membres/phare_cap_des_rosiers.htm

Ile Verte Light
Managed by the Canadian Coast
Guard
www.ileverte.net/ (in French)

La Martre Light
Managed by Municipality of La
Martre. Take highway 132 into
the village of La Martre.

Matane Light
Managed by Ville de Matane. On
Route 132 in Matane.

Pointe-à-la-Renommée Light
(418) 269-3310

Pointe-au-Père Light
(418) 724-6214
gorp.away.com/gorp/location/
Canada/quebec/trip_for.htm

Pointe-des-Monts Light
www.pointe-des-monts.com
(418) 939-2332 (summer)
(418) 589-8408 (winter)

Pot à l'Eau-de-Vie Light
(418) 867-1660
www.duvetnor.com/english/
night.htm

Seaworthy Movies

Amistad, 1997, Universal Studios
Featuring Morgan Freeman and Anthony Hopkins, this movie vividly depicts the mutiny aboard the slave ship *Amistad* and the subsequent trials.

The Black Swan, 1942, Twentieth Century Fox
Featuring Tyrone Power and Maureen O'Hara, this film depicts a former pirate who becomes governor of Jamaica and subsequently sends a former mate to rid the area of pirates.

Captain Blood, 1935, Warner Studios
In this swashbuckler featuring Errol Flynn and Olivia De Havilland, a doctor turns to a life of piracy after being wrongly imprisoned in the 1700s.

Hawaii, 1966, MGM/United Artist Studios
Featuring Julie Andrews and Max Von Sydow, this is the story of a missionary and his wife in Hawaii in the early 1900s. The movie shows Hawaii during the golden age of whaling.

Moby Dick, 1956, MGM/United Artist Studios
Featuring Gregory Peck and Richard Basehart, this is a great whaling movie that shows the seaport New Bedford, Massachusetts, in the 1800s.

Moby Dick: The True Story, Artisan Fox Video, 2002
This is a wonderful documentary from the Discovery Channel about the wreck of the whaleship *Essex*.

Mutiny on the Bounty, 1935, Warner Studios
Featuring Charles Laughton and Clark Gable, this is based on the true story of mutiny on the British ship *Bounty* in 1789.

The Bounty, 1984, MGM/United Artists
Featuring Mel Gibson and Anthony Hopkins, this is an updated version of the same story.

The Sea Hawk, 1940, Warner Studios
Featuring Errol Flynn and Brenda Marshall, this is the swashbuckling story of an English privateer.

Web Sites

Amistad America
www.amistadamerica.org
You'll enjoy a visit to this informative site about the *Amistad* mutiny; it features a reproduction of the ship *Amistad.*

BoatSafe Kids
www.boatsafe.com/kids
This is a great nautical site for kids.

Enchanted Learning Whales
www.enchantedlearning.com/subjects/whales
This site offers easy-to-understand information about whales, with drawings you can print out.

Lighthouse Depot (international listing of lighthouses).
www.lighthousedepot.com

The Mariner's Museum
www.mariner.org
Here you'll find wonderful online exhibitions on women and the sea, the art of the tattoo, lighthouses, lighthouse keepers, and more.

Maritime History on the Internet
http://ils.unc.edu/maritime
This site has links to all the important maritime sites.

The Maritime History Virtual Archives
http://pc-78-120.udac.se:8001/WWW/Nautica/Nautica.html
This is a top-rated maritime history Web site.

National Park Service
www.cr.nps.gov/maritime/lt_index.htm
This specialized site on lighthouse heritage lists U.S. lighthouses with pictures and facts about each.

New Bedford Whaling Museum
www.whalingmuseum.org
This is a great site that features concise, accurate information on American whaling.

New England Lighthouses. (Virtual guide to lighthouses.)
www.lighthouse.cc

Pirates!
www.nationalgeographic.com/features/97/pirates/maina.html
This site offers an interactive look at pirates.

Pirates! Fact and Legend
www.piratesinfo.com/main.php
If you're looking for interesting facts about pirates, this is the site for you.

Sailing Ships Page
www.infa.abo.fi/~fredrik/sships
Here you'll find a wealth of information about ships, masts, sails, and rigging.

Schooner Man: Schooner and Tall Sailing Ships
www.schoonerman.com
This is another great site with a wealth of information and numerous links about sailing ships.

Sea World in Florida
www.seaworld.org

Shanties and Sea Songs
www.rendance.org/shanty
This site features a wonderful compilation of sea chanteys and songs.

Unites States Coast Guard
www.uscg.mil/hq/g-cp/history/WEBLIGHTHOUSES/lighthouse_curricu lum.html
Visit this site and you'll find a printable packet of the story of the lighthouse containing a lot of information and pictures.

United States Merchant Marines
www.usmm.org

Whalecraft
www.whalecraft.net
This site provides comprehensive information and pictures of whaling tools.

Whale Guide
www.whaleguide.com
Listings of whale watching cruises worldwide.

WhaleNet
www.whalenet.org
This is an interactive educational Web site for students, parents, and teachers.

Index